JEEP

EIGHT DECADES FROM WILLYS TO WRANGLER

PATRICK R. FOSTER

motorbooks

ACKNOWLEDGMENTS

I would like to thank everyone who helped me with this and other books I've written, especially Cruse Moss, Jack Wildman, Bob Nixon, Vince Geraci, Frank Pascoe, Roy Lunn, Phil Payne, Jim Pappas, Ron Konopka, Denise Barton, Tom Hale, Dan Kunz, Phil Lundy, George Maddox, R. William McNealy, Gerry Meyers, Bill and Amy Tilden, and the late Roy D. Chapin Jr. If I've missed anyone, it was not intentional and I apologize in advance.

This book is dedicated to my parents, Wilfred and Liane Foster.

Brimming with creative inspiration, how-to projects, and useful information to enrich your everyday life, Quarto Knows is a favorite destination for those pursuing their interests and passions. Visit our site and dig deeper with our books into your area of interest: Quarto Creates, Quarto Cooks, Quarto Homes, Quarto Lives, Quarto Drives, Quarto Explores, Quarto Gifts, or Quarto Kids.

Inspiring | Educating | Creating | Entertaining

© 2014, 2020 Quarto Publishing Group USA Inc.
Text © 2014, 2020 Patrick R. Foster

All photographs are from the author's collection unless noted otherwise.

First published in 2014 by Motorbooks, an imprint of The Quarto Group, 100 Cummings Center, Suite 265-D, Beverly, MA 01915, USA. T (978) 282-9590 F (978) 283-2742 QuartoKnows.com

Motorbooks titles are also available at discount for retail, wholesale, promotional, and bulk purchase. For details, contact the Special Sales Manager by email at specialsales@quarto.com or by mail at The Quarto Group, Attn: Special Sales Manager, 100 Cummings Center, Suite 265-D, Beverly, MA 01915, USA.

This publication has not been prepared, approved, or licensed by Jeep.

ISBN: 978-0-7603-6655-4

Library of Congress has cataloged the previous edition as follows:

Foster, Patrick R.
  Jeep : the history of America's greatest vehicle / Patrick R. Foster.
    pages cm
  Summary: "Jeep chronicles the history of this uniquely American brand, starting with its wartime inception and moving through the 20th century, fully illustrated throughout and loaded with facts and sidebars"-- Provided by publisher.
  ISBN 978-0-7603-4585-6 (hardback)
  1. Jeep automobile--History. 2. Sport utility vehicles--United States--History. I. Title.
  TL215.J44F6495 2014
  629.222'2--dc23
                    2014006473

Editor: Darwin Holmstrom
Art Director: James Kegley
Interior Design: Kim Winscher
Additional Layout: Rebecca Pagel

On the front cover: 2020 Jeep Gladiator. *Chris Collard*

Printed in China
10 9 8 7 6 5 4 3

CONTENTS

INTRODUCTION

America's greatest vehicle is the Jeep. Created out of intense prewar competition, the Willys Jeep served in World War II as a reconnaissance car, weapons carrier, supply truck, front-line ambulance, attack vehicle, ammunition hauler, and many, many other jobs. It became indispensable to American GIs and their allies around the world.

FORGED IN WAR

IT WAS UTTER INSANITY, like being locked in a coffin: suffocating, dark, and hellish. It was the most frightening place on Earth. Lost in a dense green jungle so thick you could barely see 10 feet ahead, with bullets whizzing past, men getting hit, strange voices shouting, and shells exploding all around, it was the crazy, senseless madness of war in all its terrifying reality.

This was Guadalcanal, August 1942. The United States, which had been having the worst of the war in the Pacific, was finally getting a chance to fight back. Taking this steaming, blood-soaked island from the Japanese would be a major victory, but it would not be without cost. The Japanese were fighting back savagely.

Way out on the front lines of this impenetrable green hell, Corporal Jamie O. Sarver was suddenly shot down. Seriously wounded and losing blood fast, he realized that this might be the last day he'd ever see. He was too far forward to be carried out by his buddies, even if they could get through the storm of bullets that were flying all around. And if, by some chance, they did manage to reach him and get him to safety, he would probably bleed to death long before he got to the distant field hospital. Things were grim.

Then, suddenly, he heard the roar of an engine being pressed for all it was worth. He looked up to see a stubby, grimy Jeep charging hell-for-leather through the jungle, dodging bullets, bouncing through shell holes and chewing up the undergrowth as it stubbornly clawed its way along, its driver's face set in grim determination. Call it a miracle. The driver, who somehow wasn't hit, lifted Sarver into the Jeep and drove him to the aid station. A life was saved.

The Jeep MB was the original go-anywhere, do-anything vehicle, a workhorse for the military and a friend to the soldier.

ACROSS THE WORLD, at El Alamein, Egypt, in World War II's desert theater, Jeeps were engaged in many other spectacular feats. Perhaps the most daring was when a fleet of heavily armed Jeeps left British general Bernard Montgomery's headquarters to stage a raid on General Erwin Rommel's supply line. Traveling by night and hiding during the day, they moved in a wide arc that eventually brought them far behind German lines. There, they arrayed themselves on a hilltop overlooking a dusty road: Rommel's supply route. Within hours, a convoy of tanker trucks appeared, hauling badly needed fuel for Rommel's tanks. At a word, the Jeeps fired up their engines and came swooping down from their hiding place. Driving flat out, their heavy machine guns spitting bullets at a frantic pace, the Jeeps weaved in and out of the German column, bringing a hellish destruction with them. Within seconds, the German force was reduced to nothing more than a line of blazing trucks and dead Nazi soldiers. The Jeeps then slipped away into the darkness and made it safely back to their own lines.

Wartime Jeep adventures weren't always grim. One amusing tale is the story of two newspaper correspondents who slogged through the impenetrable jungles of Burma and India's Manipur Hills, arriving at last in Imphal with their Jeep covered in thick mud. An officer who spoke with them told them their sense of geography must have been mixed up, because, as he said, "There isn't a single road across those jungles and hills."

For many a wounded soldier, the best sight in the world was that of a Jeep coming to the rescue. The Jeep MB could claw its way through just about any kind of terrain, and the vehicles helped save the lives of many wounded soldiers by carrying them back from the front lines to forward aid stations.

"Shh," replied one of the newsmen. "Our Jeep hasn't found out about roads yet and we don't want to spoil it."

A more poignant tale came from the battlefield in Holland. Soon after a British Army column had been strafed by German warplanes, a correspondent came across a lone private crying his eyes out while sitting next to his bomb-blasted Jeep. The correspondent understood the situation immediately and offered that the solider would soon get another Jeep. Inconsolable, the private looked up with tears streaming down his face. "It ain't that, sir," he said. "You see, I loved *this* one."

Is it any wonder that GIs around the world came to love the Jeep? It was the ultimate do-it-all machine for the armed forces of the United States and her allies, and it was a faithful friend. If a GI needed hot food, he could place his

War in the South Pacific was often a nightmare, but the Jeeps helped make life just a bit easier. Here a Jeep leads troops across a blasted island landscape.

C-ration cans on the manifold of his Jeep's engine and in no time flat, he would have a steaming hot dinner. If he wanted a hot shave, he could simply drain a little water from the Jeep radiator and lather up. By attaching a belt to one wheel, a soldier could use his Jeep to power a sawmill for providing firewood or to cut boards for flooring his tent. The mighty Jeep carried men and supplies to the front lines and carried the wounded back to hospitals and aid stations. Equipped with a .50-caliber machine gun, it could be a terrifying weapon; equipped with a standard chaplain's pack, its hood served as the altar at field church services. In areas where the existing railroad stock had been destroyed, GIs fitted their Jeeps with special railroad wheels, turning them into locomotives capable of hauling a trainload of supplies. Special wide wheel additions allowed a Jeep to power its way through the deepest snow. With a radio set, it became a forward artillery

Top: This Jeep MB was one of the casualties of the invasion of Guadalcanal and a grim depiction of the horrors of war. Whether it got stuck in the gooey sand and had to be abandoned or its troops themselves were casualties is not known.

Bottom: One valiant use of the Jeep was as a combat assault vehicle. Here we see soldiers swinging into action in their early-series Jeep MB. Note that the Jeep carries a crew of three and mounts a machine gun. Note, too, the rifle standing upright in its leather carrier.

Equipped with a heavy machine gun, the Jeep was also a powerful and destructive anti-aircraft weapon.

Left: Soldiers could always have a hot meal if they had a Jeep. In this wartime picture, we see a group of GIs heating their dinner on the exhaust manifold of a Jeep. This image appeared originally as an advertisement for Campbell's soup with the title "How to pull a hot dinner out of a Jeep."

Right: Equipped with special wheels that GIs fashioned on the spot, the Jeep became a railroad engine and could haul carloads of men and supplies.

spotter and, back of the lines, a portable air traffic–control tower. Many a lonely soldier waited hopefully for the Jeep that brought in mail from home. And many a weary soldier appreciated the chance to simply get off his feet and ride in a Jeep rather than slog along in the mud.

At one airbase in Australia, Jeeps came to the rescue when it became necessary to lay some heavy electrical cable across the airdrome. Although this was typically a three-day job,

the commandant wanted it done much more quickly, so that flying operations wouldn't be interrupted. It was a group of American soldiers that came up with an idea for speeding things up: They hitched a plow to a Jeep and set off to dig a trench at 10 miles per hour. Right behind it was a second Jeep laying down the cable as it followed along. A third Jeep followed, equipped with a scraper and a roller to level the ground after the cable was in place. Instead of three days, the job was done in two hours.

American war correspondent Ernie Pyle, beloved by GIs the world over, described the Jeep this way: "Good Lord, I don't think we could carry on the war with the Jeep. It's as faithful as a dog, as strong as a mule and as agile as a goat"[1] General "Ike" Eisenhower, the U.S. supreme allied commander in Europe, claimed that the three tools that won the war were the Jeep, the Dakota airplane, and the landing craft. He listed the Jeep first. U.S. Army Chief

This Jeep has been modified with wheel extensions to help it get through deep snow.

Equipped with a light machine gun, as shown here, the Jeep could serve as a convoy escort vehicle, a fast attack vehicle, or even a portable anti-aircraft weapon.

[1] Pyle was a favorite of servicemen everywhere because of the affectionate way he wrote about them. Pyle was killed in April 1945 when his Jeep was ambushed by Japanese soldiers. He was buried in the South Pacific alongside some of the GIs he held in such high regard.

Is there any wonder that soldiers everywhere fell in love with their Jeeps? They were faithful companions that often got men through the most difficult terrain and sometimes even saved their lives. With a low-cut body, bucket seats, and a floor shift, it was as close to a sports car as most GIs had ever driven before.

Left: This photo, dated July 10, 1944, shows another load of Jeeps being readied for shipment to waiting soldiers. During the war, more than 670,000 Jeeps were produced, with the majority of them produced by Willys-Overland Corporation and the rest by Ford and Bantam Motors. There was a heavy demand for the versatile, unstoppable Jeep throughout the war.

Right: Here we see one of the most important uses of the Jeep—rushing medics to a fallen warrior. The Jeep could carry a medic and all his equipment right to the front lines and be used to evacuate the wounded.

of Staff General George C. Marshall, no minor authority on combat, called the Jeep America's greatest contribution to warfare. It was all that and more. It was the cavalry mount for a modern era.

Jeep made just about everything easier. Recon patrols were a lot less work when you could drive a Jeep rather than walk. On the march, a Jeep could carry the men's packs, carry soldiers across streams, and even provide light where there was none. Military airports

Top: Inside war-torn Europe, probably sometime in 1944: U.S. soldiers enter the bomb-blasted town of Vergato, Italy, about 40 miles southwest of Bologna. The bullet-riddled homes, rubble-filled streets, and blown-out windows testify to the ferocity of the battle to take this town. Note that the tank in the background has a plow blade attached to its front.

Bottom: When modified to carry litters, a Jeep could take three wounded men at a time back to the aid station, as this British Army Jeep demonstrates. Notice the driver has named his Jeep "Nell".

used Jeeps to tow planes around the airfield. After Europe was invaded, battle-hardened warriors learned to weld a vertical bar to the front of their Jeeps to cut any trip wires set up by the Germans to snap the necks of unsuspecting drivers.

And it was fun to drive. Besides being incredibly durable, the Willys Jeep engine offered plenty of power. With this engine, combined with bucket seats, floor shift, and low-cut sides, the Jeep was as close to a sports car as many young men ever got—and they loved to drive it, especially into town when on leave.

Everyone involved in the war overseas wanted one, and they usually got them. Willys-Overland, maker of the Jeep, sent thousands of Jeeps overseas, as did Ford Motor Company, which built the Willys Jeep under license. In all, Willys produced more than 360,000 Jeeps, while Ford built more than 277,000. Besides

the Pacific Theater, these Jeeps were shipped to Great Britain, Africa, India, and China—virtually anywhere there were forces fighting. More than 80,000 Jeeps were sent to Russia, whose army used them as a spearhead for their highly successful mobilized campaigns.

The vehicle had several nicknames, including Jeep, Peep, Blitz-Buggy, and the Soldier's Friend. GIs often bestowed personal

After the Normandy invasion, battle-hardened GIs welded wire cutters on the front of their Jeeps. The Nazis ran wires across roadways to snap the necks of unsuspecting soldiers.

names on their Jeeps as well. One Willys Jeep that saw action on Guadalcanal was dubbed "Old Faithful" by the Marines who used it. "Old Faithful" was officially retired on October 13, 1942, and enshrined in the Marines Corps Museum at Quantico, Virginia. It was awarded a Purple Heart medal for wounds received in battle—two shrapnel holes in the windshield. Another Jeep, this one named "Gramps," is the oldest surviving example of the original order of prototype or test vehicles. Made by Bantam Motors, it's currently housed at the Smithsonian.

Songs were written about the Jeep; "Little Bo Peep Has Lost Her Jeep" was the most popular. There was a pretty good movie, too, titled *Four Jills in a Jeep*, based on the experiences of four actresses entertaining troops during the war. Another movie, this one postwar, was *Four in a Jeep*, a drama about four sergeants on patrol in a Jeep.

A popular movie during World War II was *Four Jills in a Jeep*, starring Kay Francis, Martha Raye, Mitzi Mayfair, and the gorgeous Carole Landis. In the film, the four women play themselves as they travel from one war location to another entertaining the troops. Also appearing in this fun little movie are Phil Silvers, Dick Haymes, Betty Grable, George Jessel, and Carmen Miranda.

The versatile Willys Jeep was light and compact enough to fit into an airplane or glider, as seen here, and could even be parachuted into action. Gliders like these were used extensively in the D-Day invasion.

Back home, hundreds of clubs, civic groups, and other organizations held bake sales and raffles to raise funds to buy more Jeeps. Here we see a fairly typical group celebrating their contribution of a new Jeep for the war effort.

Entertainer Joe E. Brown greets Chinese children from the wheel of a Jeep. Brown had a special reason for feeling proud of the Jeep: He was born near Toledo, Ohio, where most of the wartime Jeeps came from.

Back at home, Jeep was nearly as popular as it was at the front. Civic organizations sponsored wartime bond drives with a ride in a Jeep as a reward. Cub Scouts and Rotarians and every other type of club held bake sales and pasta dinners to raise money that was donated to the government to buy extra Jeeps for the war effort.

The number of celebrities, politicians, world and civic leaders, and other VIPs who had their pictures taken in Jeeps is impossible to number, but to name just a few: Humphrey Bogart, Rosalind Russell, Marilyn Monroe, Elvis Presley, Queen Elizabeth I, King Farouk of Egypt, Franklin Delano Roosevelt, Winston Churchill, and Chiang Kai-shek. The number of times Jeep vehicles have been used in the movies is plainly incalculable.

Top: One of the greatest U.S. presidents, Franklin Delano Roosevelt, is seen reviewing troops from an army Jeep. Roosevelt was president when the war began and delivered the initial announcement of the commencement of hostilities on December 8, 1941, the day after the Japanese sneak attack on Pearl Harbor.

Bottom: Two of the United Kingdom's wartime leaders are shown here in a Lend Lease Jeep: General Bernard Law Montgomery, seated in the rear and wearing a beret, and British Prime Minister Winston Churchill, seen lighting a cigar.

Top: Thousands of women served in the military during World War II and a good number of them served as drivers for officers. Here we see one such soldier, checking under the hood of her Jeep, probably in England. Note the overseas (or garrison) cap she is wearing.

Bottom: The U.S. Army has produced many outstanding soldiers, but there were few braver than Teddy Roosevelt Jr., son of former president Theodore Roosevelt. When he learned that he would not be allowed to take part in the D-Day invasion, he successfully petitioned his superiors to be allowed to go in with the first wave of troops. He was 56 years old when he became one of the generals to lead the assault on bloody Utah Beach on D-Day. Old for that kind of service, and partly crippled by arthritis, he needed a cane to walk. On the beach, he steadied the young soldiers with his calm, fearless demeanor. Miraculously, he was not wounded during the invasion, during which he displayed extraordinary bravery under fire. He is shown here shortly after the D-day invasion in his Jeep, which he nicknamed the "Rough Rider". Sadly, this gallant man died of a heart attack shortly after this photo was taken.

The Jeep was ideally designed. Small and light, it could be manhandled out of any mishap, whether it was getting stuck in the mud, being overturned by a bomb blast, or getting over an oversized log. It was small enough to fit in an airplane, light enough to be parachuted into action, powerful enough to climb the steepest hills, economical enough to get by on a small diet of fuel, and brawny enough to handle a few bullet holes and shrapnel with ease. It could tow a howitzer across a beach or through

a jungle and go back for more ammunition when needed. The Jeep was built tough, and if anything did go wrong it was simple to fix. It could plow snow, haul food supplies, power a well pump, and even dig trenches. It was and is a miracle machine, and it is America's greatest vehicle of all time.

And yet it almost didn't come to be. Before 1941, there was no Jeep, or any vehicle even remotely like it; there was only a vague yearning by the military for some sort of vehicle that could be used for reconnaissance on and off the road, haul supplies, and possibly be used to mount a weapon. Different vehicle designs were tried, none successfully. And when the army finally discovered the sturdy little mule of a vehicle they were looking for, they almost rejected it because they thought it weighed a little too much. In the end, 7 or 9 ounces of metal made the difference between the army having a Jeep—or not.

Top: Another photo of President Franklin Roosevelt, this time with naval officers. A victim of polio, Roosevelt could only walk with crutches, but despite his handicap he was an active leader of his country during the war and was beloved by millions of Americans. Sadly, he would not survive the war.

Bottom Left: One of the great treats for the victorious American troops in Paris was to drive out to see the Eiffel Tower in their Jeeps. Thousands of soldiers who had never left the farm before were able to see Europe, though of course they had to fight most of the way through it.

Top: It took great courage to overcome one's fears and drive off a landing craft under fire, but many a young man had to do it. Notice the snorkels mounted on the Jeeps; these are for fording deep water.

Bottom: In addition to Jeeps, Willys produced a wide variety of critical products for the war effort. In this December 1944 photo, Willys workers are shown assembling the new "robot bombs" similar to the Nazi V-2 rockets.

Opposite page
Bottom Right: A proud scene as American soldiers enter the newly liberated city of Paris. Ecstatic Parisian girls swarmed the American GIs, kissing them and shouting "Bienvenue aux Jeeps!" ("Welcome to the Jeeps!"). After a bloody campaign, the Americans wrested control of the French capital from the Nazis.

CHAPTER 1

Here's the first Jeep ever made: the Bantam prototype scout car. Its designer, Karl Probst, is seen in shirtsleeves leaning against the rear-mounted spare tire. Note the front fenders are cycle-type, probably taken from a Bantam passenger car. This vehicle no longer exists, though a replica of it has been built.

1940–1941

A LEGEND IS BORN

MILITARY PLANNERS OF 1939–1941 were a lonely, sometimes frustrated lot. At the time most Americans considered the ongoing war overseas to be a European problem, or an Asian hotspot, not anything to concern the United States. However, U.S. Army planners realized that once a fire starts it's likely to spread, in this case, engulfing the world. They could see that the war was steadily advancing across the globe. Overall, America's peacetime army was suffering from severely restricted budgets and a general sense of complacency. The public didn't want to get involved in an overseas war, and that was that. With limited funds and the knowledge that the time for preparation could be very short, these planners began to prepare the services for a war that only they could see.

They looked at strategies, logistics, and the tools of war. One thing they knew had to change was the army's reliance on the horse and mule to transport equipment. World War I had demonstrated the effectiveness of motorized transportation and the amazing ability of four-wheel drive in tough going. During that war, motorized trucks were put into service by the thousands and showed they could haul more freight more miles than any team of mules could hope to. In addition, certain vehicles with four-wheel drive, mainly the Nash Quad four-wheel-drive trucks, could haul heavy guns through mud and snow that would stop even the most determined two-wheel-drive truck. And it was found that for light work, or for front line use, a conventional two- or four-wheel-drive truck was usually too big. So the planners began to think of a smaller, lighter vehicle.

Here we see one of the Howie Machine Gun Carriers, also known as the "Bellyflopper." Captain Robert Howie created this design as an attack machine, low and sleek, that could slip through tall grass and add a lot of firepower to an assaulting force. Although it had possibilities, in the end it proved impractical.

FOR YEARS THE ARMY had also wanted to find a small vehicle that could be used for reconnaissance and messenger service. They tried motorcycles, both with and without side cars, and they learned that two- or three-wheel machines soon got hopelessly bogged down in sand and muck. They also tried a fleet of Ford Model T's stripped down to the bare essentials. These light touring cars performed fairly well, but the minute any additional weight was added—such as armoring or a machine gun—they got too heavy for cross-country going. In addition, they weren't rugged enough for the often-severe off-road use for which they would be needed. In 1932 the Infantry Board tried another light car, ordering testing on an Austin, a tiny British car being built in Butler, Pennsylvania. The diminutive Austin's purchase price for the army was a mere $286.75. Although it did fairly well in testing, the Austin too was not rugged enough. But it did influence the army's thinking in what it might expect in the performance of a small, purpose-built vehicle.

At the same time that the military was sorting through the problems of a light reconnaissance vehicle, it was also trying to come up with a light, portable weapons carrier that could be used in close support of infantry because the army's big .50-caliber machine guns were too heavy for soldiers to carry long distances. They first tried using the heavy trucks of the day, but these were simply too big for cross-country use and provided too large a profile, making them sitting ducks for enemy fire. The planners saw that what was needed was a lightweight, low-profile four-wheel-drive vehicle that could travel off-road as well as on-road.

Some interesting designs were tried out. Army Captain Robert G. Howie devised a vehicle that he hoped would fit the needs of the various branches of the service. He came up with what was officially called the Howie Machine Gun carrier, but that was quickly dubbed the "Belly Flopper." Howie and Master Sergeant M. C. Wiley built a handmade

This is a very rare photo of the Bantam Jeep prototype. This vehicle performed very well in military testing and is the great granddaddy of all Jeeps.

prototype of Howie's design, in which two men lay belly down on a small four-wheel platform powered by an Austin four-cylinder engine and featuring an Austin radiator, steering gear, and other components (reportedly taken from the Austin car the army purchased in 1932). The tiny vehicle was steered via tiller.

Performance was surprisingly good. The Howie machine could run 28 miles per hour and its ultra-low silhouette helped hide the men driving it. The Belly Flopper could mount a .50-caliber machine gun and could race practically undetected through the underbrush while attacking the enemy's forward positions. But the Belly Flopper had several disadvantages: With its ultra-low ground clearance and lack of springs, it couldn't be driven far, so it would have to be hauled to battle in a truck. It lacked four-wheel drive, and it couldn't carry a load other than the machine gun. The military men went back to consider other possibilities.

What these soldiers needed was a vehicle capable of reconnaissance work, like the Austin, as well as being able to carry a heavy weapon, like the Belly Flopper. The Austin reconnaissance car could be made into a good gun platform if it was beefed up considerably,

but without four-wheel drive it still wouldn't perform to the service's needs. Initially the men were in favor of a light pickup truck converted to four-wheel drive; several were tested and, although they performed much better than the heavy trucks had done, they were nearly as costly and not really suitable for command and reconnaissance purposes. And again, the vehicle silhouette was too high, making it an easy target. Overall, it was simply more vehicle than the army needed.

Finally, in 1940, the chief of infantry decided to see if any American companies could design a vehicle that would fit the multipurpose role the military needed. He settled on a set of design

During testing at Camp Holabird, Maryland, the Bantam prototype Jeep wore a license plate from the engineering department. Notice the simplicity of the area under the hood.

specifications for a vehicle that could do all three tasks: be small enough for reconnaissance and command functions, be able to haul men and supplies long distances, and be sturdy enough to carry a machine gun. They wanted a vehicle that was no more than 36 inches tall at the cowl, weighing between 750 and 1,000 pounds, with cross-country and grade-climbing capability equal to the army's heavy cargo trucks, a .30-caliber machine gun mount, the ability to carry that gun along with 3,000 rounds of ammunition, and with seating capacity for at least two men. Naturally, it also had to be equipped with four-wheel drive.

When the specifications were sent to the quartermaster general for comment, the QG's

opinion was that the program really should be placed under the responsibility of his office. He also suggested that the army's vehicle testing center at Camp Holabird, Maryland, investigate the possibility of using light passenger cars built by American Bantam, successor to the American Austin company. In June 1940 a special subcommittee met at Bantam's production facilities in Butler, Pennsylvania (the same place where the Austin car had once been built) to discuss the possibilities of Bantam supplying the various services with vehicles. The committee wanted to evaluate the Bantam car as well as the facilities that would build it. Several of Bantam's cars then demonstrated their on- and off-road abilities. The Bantams incorporated several improvements over the earlier Austins, and they performed well. To test the vehicle's structural strength, a bare chassis was weighted down with 4,500 pounds of sand; there was no damage. The military men were impressed.

The Bantam executives were pleased and more than a little relieved. Since the formation of the company in 1935, made possible by buying the former American Austin Car Company out of bankruptcy, the firm had found little success in the car business. Even though they had greatly improved the design of the renamed

Top: The Jeep could do just about anything. Though designed to be a scout car and able to carry a heavy machine gun, testing proved it could haul light artillery as well. Notice the World War I–style helmets these GIs are wearing. Early in the war, the army changed to the more familiar full bucket-style helmet.

Bottom: The Bantam prototype was driven extensively all over the U.S. Army test grounds, resulting in loose body panels, a bent frame, broken shock absorber, and several other failures. Despite the problems, the army knew it had a winner in the Jeep.

Austin car, and restyled it as well, the American public remained indifferent. Plainly, the public just couldn't be convinced to buy a small car, at least not one as tiny as the Bantam. By the time American Bantam began angling for the military contract, the company was in dire financial straits. It's only hope of salvation was to win the contract. If it didn't, it would almost certainly go out of business.

Although the Bantam executives were highly encouraged by the test results, the discussion that followed sometime afterward brought them back down to earth. The committee notified them that they would be interested in purchasing vehicles from Bantam if the body was replaced by one with low lines, three bucket seats, a folding windshield, and a low silhouette. If the vehicle had four-wheel drive, it would also have a two-speed transfer case, a front-axle disconnect feature, and more engine power, and if it was equipped with full floating axles, it would also feature hydraulic brakes, an oil-bath air cleaner, and blackout lighting. Some days later came further specifications. The vehicle could weigh no more than 1,200 pounds, have a wheelbase of not more than 75 inches, and be capable of

at least 50 miles per hour on a hard surface. The committee then sent a recommendation that the Quartermaster Corps be charged with the vehicle's development and procurement.

The secretary of war authorized an expenditure of $175,000 for the purchase of 70 test vehicles. They were to be ready in time for the army's late summer 1940 maneuvers, if at all possible. The Cavalry also wanted eight of the vehicles to be equipped with four-wheel steering.

Bantam, knowing the figure allocated for the purchase, offered to build the 70 test vehicles for $2,500 each, a total cost of $175,000. The quartermaster refused to accept this, feeling the vehicle should go out to bid in order to obtain the lowest price possible.

No vehicle of this type existed so whoever would get the final contract would have to design the vehicle from the ground up. It was expected that the first vehicle would be tested and refined before production of the additional vehicles occurred. Accordingly, invitations to bid were sent out to 135 manufacturers, including automobile and truck builders, along with specialty firms that produced vehicle bodies, chassis, or major components. It was the

Army testers were told to beat the Jeep prototypes until something broke. This is the Ford Pygmy prototype.

largest number of manufacturers ever contacted for any single motor vehicle contract for the army. The military no doubt expected to receive significant interest in the project because, after all, $175,000 was a lot of money. But in the end only two companies put in proposals for producing the vehicle. Interestingly, the two bidders were small-car builders Bantam Motors and Willys-Overland.

Basically, what these two companies had in common was poverty; both sold cars that were smaller than standard size and both were suffering from minimal sales. Both felt

they needed the military contract to bring in badly needed cash. Of the two, Willys-Overland was in better shape financially, although it wasn't healthy. Willys had earned a small profit in 1937 but since then had consistently lost money. Bantam, on the other hand, was nearing bankruptcy. Both companies also happened to be the last two automakers in America who offered four-cylinder passenger cars.

The reason why there weren't more bidders was simply that the contract called for the impossible. To build a rugged vehicle with room for three and with four-wheel drive, yet with a weight limit of 1,300 pounds might have been possible using new, undeveloped alloys, yet the military stressed that it wanted standard components used to the greatest extent possible. The specs also called for the vehicle to be capable of hauling at least 600 pounds, or nearly half its own weight. Those goals were simply beyond the metallurgy and engineering technology of the day. In addition, few companies anywhere had any kind of experience with four-wheel drive. It was a rarely used technology. Besides

that, the winning bidder would have only 49 days in which to design, engineer, build, test, and deliver the prototype. Car companies of the day usual allotted two to three years to develop a new model, not a month and a half. Even if the winning bidder could produce a new car in that time, the company would have a mere 26 days in which to build the other 69 pilot models of the approved design, meanwhile incorporating any changes or enhancements dictated by the army. In other words, it was a contract that only a desperate company, one whose existence depended on getting the job, would even bother trying to win. Luckily for the army, it found not one but two such desperate companies.

Right after the subcommittee's visit, the military had shown Bantam its list of preliminary specifications for what it wanted. Although it called for a vehicle different from the Bantam production cars, Bantam president Frank Fenn felt confident that his firm could meet those targets by designing a new vehicle that used many Bantam components. With most of its employees long since gone, Bantam had no engineers left on staff to tackle the project, so to create a bid it called on noted freelance engineer Karl Probst, who had a firm in Detroit. Bantam executives assumed he would jump at the opportunity, but he turned them down flat. It's really not hard to figure out why; Bantam itself had no money to pay Probst unless the company won the contract, so the best Bantam could offer him was a contingency fee. If the army chose his design, fine; but if it didn't, he would get no pay.

"The year 1940 was a time to work and pay your bills, not a time to consider jobs with no guaranteed salary," Probst later recalled. "But 1940 was also a time when you could hear the nervous joke: Hitler has ordered 10,000 tanks from General Motors. Hitler said, 'Never

mind shipping them; we'll pick them up on our way through Detroit.' " After some urging from Fenn, Probst agreed to think it over some more.

Fenn, still believing the contract would call for a vehicle mechanically similar to his Bantam cars, called Probst on Monday, July 15, 1940, saying he expected to receive the army's final specifications within a few days. Probst remained noncommittal; however, the very next day he received a phone call from Art Brandt, a member of the National Defense Advisory Committee, which was headed up by former GM president Bill Knudsen, a well-admired industry legend. His message: Knudsen was asking Probst to put aside private concerns because this military project was vital to the country's defense efforts. "We think you can

The Bantam prototype is seen here as it underwent testing at Camp Holabird, Maryland, in September 1940.

An improved version of the Bantam scout car called the Mark II went into production and many of them were sent to Lend Lease allies, mainly Russia.

do this job faster than the big companies," said Brandt, adding, "Financing will be available if you produce a vehicle to specs." Thankfully, Probst was a patriot; despite the disadvantages of the contract, he immediately agreed to create a design for Bantam to use in its bidding.

On Wednesday, July 17, Fenn received the army's final bid specifications, which Probst would need to design the new vehicle. But when Fenn looked over the specs, his heart sank. Sure, the army had said they wanted more power, but what the specs now called for was double the power his engine offered. Frantic, he called Probst. "Karl," he hollered into the phone, "we got the formal bids. Somebody made one 'little' change; they raised the minimum horsepower from the Bantam's 20 to 40. You know what this means. Our transmission won't take it, our axles won't take it, frame, suspension. . . . We'll have to jack up the horn button so you can design a new car underneath."

The specifications still called for an overall weight of a mere 1,300 pounds and a delivery time of just 49 days for the prototype. Fenn was nervous and depressed, but Probst calmed him down saying, "Well, we can produce design drawings faster than our competitors. Of course, we can't make that weight target, but neither can anyone else."

From long experience designing cars and components, Probst knew that what the army was asking for was an impossible goal. His mind made up, Probst left that day for Butler, Pennsylvania. He stopped along the way at Spicer Manufacturing Company in Toledo, Ohio, to discuss axles with their representatives. Since the Bantam's stock axles couldn't stand up under the strain of the extra power called for in the specs, he would have to find something else. He was in luck; Spicer had another axle that might work, one used on the Studebaker Champion. The Champion was a 65-horsepower car, so there would be plenty of reserve strength

In this rare photo we see chassis details of the Bantam Mk II. Precious few of these vehicles have survived.

Another view of the Bantam Mk II shows the flat front fenders the company adopted. The Bantams generally performed better than the Ford in testing, but not as well as the Willys.

in a 40-horsepower vehicle. With that settled, Probst turned his 1938 Buick eastward toward Butler, mentally putting together components as he drove. He reached town around midnight.

Probst reported in at Bantam the following morning, Thursday, July 18. He looked over the bid specifications, which included a rough outline drawing of what the car might look like. Probst later recalled that the outline: "… [It] even looked something like the car that I subsequently designed, but outlines are not design." At 1 p.m. Probst sat down at a drafting table to begin work on what would become the most important military vehicle ever, something that would become legendary.

Since there was no practical way to boost the Bantam engine to 40 horsepower, Probst had to find another engine. Choices were few, but he decided on a good one, a Continental four that delivered 45-horsepower. The bid called for the design to be presented to the army no later than the morning of July 22, just four days hence. Probst could tell by that short deadline that this was an urgent, high-priority project for the

army and something vitally important. Between that and the fact that Bantam Motors' existence was relying on him, Probst carried a lot of responsibility on his shoulders. He worked at his customary smooth, steady pace, finishing up for the day at 11 p.m. The next day he showed up for work at 7 a.m. and worked until evening, finishing the design in 18 hours. Exhilarated but tired, Probst headed into town to take in a new film starring Hedy Lamarr.

Probst spent that Saturday preparing weight and cost estimates. He concluded that the vehicle would weigh about 1,850 pounds, or 550 pounds

over the army's weight bogey. The next day, a Sunday, Probst met with Bantam officials to fill out the necessary bid forms and prepare the blueprints. With the company in more dire straits than ever, Bantam bid $2,445.51 per vehicle, for a total of $171,185.75.

As soon as the bid forms were completed the men took the long drive to Baltimore for a late-night meeting with Bantam's Washington representative, retired Navy Commander Charles Payne, at a local hotel. Payne was the person who would actually present the bid to the military, but when he looked over the bids he stopped at the section regarding weight. Probst, wishing to be completely honest, had put in his estimate of 1,850 pounds. No, said Payne, we can't go in with that. He explained that if they didn't change the weight estimate to

1,300 pounds, then under military bidding rules Bantam's bid would be automatically rejected. "We've got to bid it at 1,300 pounds," he said. "We'll get it revised after we get the contract."

This created a new problem: The completed bid forms could not be altered, Bantam did not have another copy, and it was nearly midnight. But the resourceful Payne called up an army buddy at Holabird, who sent over the needed blank forms. Then he told the hotel manager to get a stenographer over to the hotel at once. The woman arrived around 3:30 a.m. and got to work typing out the forms. By daybreak the documents were ready, with a new weight estimate of 1,273 pounds, well under the army's goal. Around 8:30 on the morning of July 22, Fenn, Probst, and Payne arrived at Camp Holabird, exhausted but happy. They had overcome many obstacles and at last the pay-off was at hand.

It was hot that morning, more than 100 degrees in the shade. The Bantam people looked around and noticed that representatives from Ford, Crosley Motors, and Willys-Overland were present. Of these, only Willys had a prepared bid and it paled in comparison to the Bantam package. Willys' chief engineer, Delmar "Barney" Roos, had hastily put together a time and cost estimate but no blueprints or plans. Willys was allowed to bid even with

Top: More rough off-road testing of the Bantam Mk II. Notice the soldier in the rear seat, whose helmet is falling off.

Bottom: This image shows two Bantam MK IIs undergoing testing at Fort Knox, Kentucky. The soldiers are dressed in cold-weather gear.

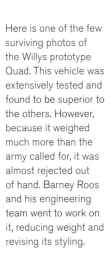

One of the best engineers this country has ever produced was Delmar "Barney" Roos. Nicknamed after his childhood hero racecar driver Barney Oldfield, Roos came up with the design that became the standard for the military Jeep.

this skimpy package, but it obviously hadn't put much time in the proposal. The Crosley and Ford representatives apparently were just observing the bidding.

A tense half hour passed, and then it was time for the army to come back to announce the winner. With little preamble, Major Herbert J. Lawes, in charge of purchasing and contracts, announced to the assembled men that Willys-Overland Motors had submitted the low bid, but he quickly added that Willys was unable to produce a running pilot car in the required 49 days. Willys apparently said it needed 75 days to do that. Since the army wanted this new vehicle pronto, there was a penalty of $5 per day for every day past 49 days, and that alone had made the Bantam bid lower. Fenn, Probst, and Payne breathed a sigh of relief. Now all they had to do was build the thing in 49 days or less. Time was

of the essence; the army would exact a hefty penalty for every day that Bantam was late in delivering the first vehicle.

Here is one of the few surviving photos of the Willys prototype Quad. This vehicle was extensively tested and found to be superior to the others. However, because it weighed much more than the army called for, it was almost rejected out of hand. Barney Roos and his engineering team went to work on it, reducing weight and revising its styling.

What the military didn't know was that even as the Bantam team stood there at Camp Holabird they weren't sure they could make the deadline. But they had decided to go ahead with the bid and not worry about penalties. "What do penalties matter to a company that is, in effect, bankrupt?" Probst noted. On July 25, 1940, Bantam was officially awarded a contract for the new military vehicle, with the contract dated August 5, 1940. The countdown clock began ticking.

As soon as he got back to Butler, Probst and a small crew of Bantam workers got to work assembling the vehicle. It wasn't a matter of picking components from Bantam's parts bins; most of the vehicle was completely different from the Bantam car. For instance, since the Bantam four-cylinder engine had been replaced by the 45-horsepower Continental four, Bantam's axles, as already noted, wouldn't work either, so the Studebaker Champion axles would have to be modified to fit. And this caused the first delay because Spicer was having problems adapting the axle for use in a four-wheel-drive vehicle. Spicer promised to put a team on the job of trying to figure out a way to make the axle fit, but it would take time, and time was precious. Besides the axles, a new transmission also had to be sourced that could handle the extra power. It would be provided by Warner Gear. Spicer would supply the four-wheel-drive transfer case.

The Bantam team worked night and day on the prototype. Beginning with the frame, they installed the engine, transmission, and rear axle. A body was made up of mostly new, fairly flat steel panels, along with basically stock Bantam front fenders from the parts bin. The cowl and hood were modified Bantam units. But the days clicked off and still the vehicle had no front drive; Spicer was still trying to adapt the Studebaker axle. Probst grew discouraged as the deadline loomed closer and closer. Three weeks before the September 23 deadline, he called Art Brandt

Another view of the Willys Quad with its creator, Barney Roos. In the end, Roos and his team were able to reduce the weight of the Willys vehicle to where it met army specifications, if only barely.

Here we see the third iteration of the Bantam four-wheel drive, this one dubbed the BRC-40, which stood for Bantam Reconnaissance Car, 40 horsepower. Hundreds of these were sent to the Russian forces; do any still exist over there?

Here we see a Bantam BRC-40 in a sling being lifted aboard a ship for transport to the war front, probably Russia, since that appears to be where most of the Bantams went.

to say they weren't going to make it; the axle problem wasn't getting solved.

Miraculously, in the end all the various problems were worked out. Spicer found a way to adapt the axle for four-wheel drive and delivered a prototype on Sunday, September 15, clearing away the final bottleneck. Probst and his team quickly got to work installing it on the chassis. With just eight days left to the deadline, the finishing work began. Probst notified his suppliers that they could come to the Butler plant and have one hour each to test drive the prototype, and that test day had to be Sunday September 22, just one day before the deadline.

The Bantam prototype was a squat, low-slung bug of a car, with a barebones, purpose-built appearance to both the interior and exterior. It had a scooped-out door opening, cycle front fenders, a tall windshield, and a rounded hood and grille. It was like nothing that had ever been seen before, and it looked ready for combat. The Bantam team was pleased with their handiwork. Someone filled the gas tank and Karl Probst climbed in behind the wheel. Starting it up, he headed for the base of a 45-degree grade. Shifting into four-wheel drive, he powered up the incline with ease, a broad smile breaking out on his face. "Whatever it is," he told Bantam factory manager Harold Crist, "it's a performer." Some adjustments were made, then the suppliers came and tested the vehicle, and they too were pleasantly surprised at how well it performed.

The next morning Probst and Harold Crist were to deliver the vehicle to Camp Holabird, nearly 300 miles away. Incredibly, rather than ship the precious one-of-a-kind vehicle in an enclosed truck, they decided to drive it the whole distance; doing it that way, they figured, would give them time to break in the new

engine properly and see if any problems popped up. Initially, Probst kept the speed down to break the engine in slowly, as was the practice back then. But as the hours went by and the miles slowly peeled off, he gradually began to drive faster and faster. By early afternoon the two men began worrying about making it to the camp by the 5 p.m. deadline and Probst was driving the little buggy flat out. Probst and Crist didn't roll into Holabird until 4:30 p.m., with just 30 minutes to spare. Probst recalled seeing a headline in a local paper: "Japanese Invade Indochina."

Major Lawes was there waiting. After talking a few minutes with Probst and Crist, he climbed into the vehicle and immediately headed out for the army proving grounds. Lawes placed a lot of faith in proving ground testing, the rougher the better. He took the little vehicle on a short, rough run through Holabird's punishing off-road course. When he was done, he drove back to Probst and Crist. Climbing out, he paused to

When the Willys Quad underwent a complete revision designed to lower its weight to army specs, it emerged looking quite different and was renamed the Willys MA. Here we see one of the Willys MAs at Fort Ord, California, with movie actor Wallace Beery sitting in the passenger seat. Beery was on location for the filming of *The Bugle Sounds*, an MGM drama about the mechanized cavalry. Also starring in the film was the beautiful Donna Reed.

render a judgment for posterity: "I have driven every unit the services have purchased for the last 20 years," he said. "I can judge them in 15 minutes. This vehicle is going to be absolutely outstanding. *I believe this unit will make history.*"

But the little Bantam still wasn't in the clear. One general, rubbing his chin, asked the toughest question: "How much does it weigh?" That put Probst on the spot. As the designer, he knew the vehicle could never make the army's 1,300-pound specification. But if he answered truthfully, all his work might go down the drain with the army rejecting the Bantam for being overweight. Probst decided to take the high road.

"Less fuel, oil, and water," he said, "this vehicle weighs 1,840 pounds. We'll probably have to add another 30 to 50 pounds to strengthen weaknesses that will show up in your tests." There was an awkward silence. The army had clearly said it wanted a 1,300-pound vehicle and here was the Bantam prototype weighing 540 pounds more than that, with its own designer stating that the weight would probably go *up* a little further on production models. More silence.

Then in one of the most glorious moments in military history, a cavalry general stepped forth to say, "If two men can take it out of a ditch, we need it." The officer was a big man, 6 feet, 2 inches and weighing 250 pounds. He strode over to the Bantam and, grunting with the exertion, lifted the back end of the little scout car off the ground. He turned to the others and nodded his approval. By that single, spur of the moment action, he saved the day for Bantam.

Probst and the Bantam men were free now to go back to Butler to build the rest of the 70-vehicle order. While they were working on that job, testing of the prototype continued. It was ruthless; testers ended up bending the frame and knocking several parts loose, including shift rails and taillights, and there were worn gears and broken shock absorbers as well, but overall the army men were extremely pleased. Probst was right; the Bantam was a performer, like nothing the military had ever seen before.

The 70 pilot cars were completed on time and were dispersed to various camps for in-service testing. Eight of the vehicles were equipped with four-wheel steering, and although this worked out fairly well, the quartermaster

Another view of the awesome Willys MA. In tests, the Willys continued to outshine the other two entries and in time won the contract to become the standard for light military vehicles. The Willys hood and front would be changed to the Ford style during production.

rejected the idea because it would complicate servicing the vehicles and would call for more variation in a product that the military needed to be standardized. More important than even that, having four-wheel steering would call for two more constant-velocity joints per vehicle, and the CV joints were a difficult, hard-to-get priority part, just about the only serious bottleneck the program still faced.

But meanwhile, the army brass were having second thoughts. Since this program was so vitally important, they wanted to make sure they were buying the best vehicle possible. They had been talking about ordering additional vehicles from Bantam but were worried that if a crisis came—in other words, a full-blown war—the little company wouldn't be able to produce enough machines to meet demand. In addition, they felt it prudent to have at least one other company also build the vehicles, figuring that a two-supplier system would provide additional safety against shortages. They were aware of the possibility that in the upcoming war a manufacturer's plant could be sabotaged by enemy spies, so they wanted a back-up plant on hand. The army decided to open the bidding for additional vehicles to Willys-Overland, which

had tried to win the initial contract and had considerable small-vehicle expertise, and to Ford Motor Company, which to this point had done nothing but observe the bidding and testing.

The reason Ford was included was the company's tremendous production capacity meant that they could turn out vehicles by the hundreds of thousands at short notice. But besides that, within the military hierarchy there was a definite prejudice against Bantam and in favor of Ford. Bantam was seen as too small a company and in too precarious a financial shape while Ford vehicles were well-loved and the company itself was one of the most

Jeep in Action, Camp Pickett, Va.

Here's another view of the Willys MA, an action shot taken at Camp Pickett, Virginia. Notice the old-style helmet the soldier is wearing. And where is the driver?

successful in history. With Ford there would be no doubts about the ability to fill orders. So in November of that year contracts were given to Willys and Ford to produce pilot cars to challenge the Bantam model. Both Willys and Ford were shown copies of the Bantam's plans, and engineers were allowed to inspect and take measurements of the Bantam prototype. Then each went back to their respective engineering labs to design their own vehicle. Ford accordingly

came up with its version of a reconnaissance car, which it dubbed the Pigmy, while Willys-Overland came up with a vehicle it called the Quad, a small four-wheel-drive vehicle like the others, of which it reportedly built two, one with regular steering and one with four-wheel steering, though actual photographs showing the two together apparently don't exist. The army accepted the prototypes and began testing them alongside the recently built Bantam pilot cars, which were dubbed the Bantam Mark II because they incorporated the improvements suggested by early trial tests.

The next phase of testing was serious, comprehensive, and arduous. Vehicles were rated competitively for power, ride, comfort, smoothness, and ruggedness, and ability to climb hills, ford streams, and run off-road. They were tested for top speed, fuel economy, and towing ability. They were run across fields, ditches, and up and down mountains, and often

A Willys MA undergoing deep water testing in 1941 with a Willys engineer at the wheel. The little Jeep proved it could go just about anywhere.

More testing by Willys engineers: In this dramatic shot the Willys crests a hill with all four wheels off the ground.

What better way to celebrate Christmas in the army than with Santa driving into camp in his Willys MA? Many such silly press photos were released in the days before the war.

they were run until something broke. Then notes would be made, repairs done, appropriate people notified, after which it was back to the test grounds. As all this was being done, testers began to realize that no single vehicle was superior in all ways; each offered features or performance that was a cut above the others.

The Willys Quad prototypes enjoyed several advantages. Mainly, though, their power was the biggest differentiator. Years earlier, the Willys four-cylinder engine had earned a reputation for low power, unreliability, and short life. This unfortunate reputation had hurt Willys' sales efforts, so in 1939 engineering vice president Barney Roos and assistant Floyd Kishline set to work to redesign the engine. Willys had no money to engineer an all-new powerplant, so the goal was to eliminate all the problems with the existing engine and turn it into a sturdy, reliable powerplant. Roos was determined to make the little four more powerful, smoother, quieter, and absolutely bulletproof. He and Kishline redesigned the block, cylinder head, carburetor, intake and exhaust manifolds, valves, water pump, bearings, pistons, air cleaner, and much, much more, testing the engines at full throttle to see

what the improvement was. Horsepower shot up from 48 to 60 horsepower, and durability went up substantially. Prior to the redesign, a stock Willys four would usually burn out in about four hours when run at the maximum speed for any great length of time. But by the time Roos was done, he'd gotten the engine to go 100 hours or more at peak rpm with no damage and with much greater smoothness. By then the Willys four-cylinder engine was the most powerful and most durable four in America, which now made the Quad the most powerful of the three contenders.

The Ford Pygmy was a decent enough vehicle, but its engine was an unrefined unit developing just 46 horsepower, or 1 horsepower more than the Bantam. The Ford was more than 200 pounds heavier than the Bantam, however, so its performance lagged that of both the Bantam and Willys. The problem was that Ford no longer offered four-cylinder engines in its passenger car line so it had to use an engine from a Ford tractor, and it plainly was second rate. But the Ford vehicle got high marks for fit and finish, and the army testers soon realized the Ford's flat hood and fenders were a better design because the hood could be used as a table for spreading

Here we see the revised Ford prototype called the GP. It was an improvement over the Pygmy but could not compete with the Willys MA.

out maps, while the flat fenders could serve as seats for carrying extra soldiers in a pinch.

The Bantam scored high points for its ease of handling and light weight. It also turned in the best fuel economy of the three vehicles. Willys had the best ground clearance and best hill-climbing ability, though the Bantam was also a good hill climber. Willys also accelerated better than the others and had a higher top speed, but the Willys engine was much heavier than the others, so the entire vehicle was heavy—2,520 pounds versus the Ford's 2,150 pounds and the Bantam's svelte 1,940 pounds. The army was not at all happy about the Willys heft and let the company know that the final standard weight specification would be well under that of the

Willys. However, its performance was so good the army decided to give Willys, along with Ford and Bantam, a contract for 1,500 more vehicles. The 4,500 total vehicles would be tested further and from that a winner would be chosen that would get the big contract everyone wanted.

Willys' Barney Roos realized that although they had a small contract for vehicles, they would not win the big contract unless the Quad was redesigned for less weight. That was crucial. Luckily Roos was a specialist in getting weight out of small cars, so he and his engineering team set to work going through the Quad piece by piece with the goal of cutting at least 300 pounds from what was already a barebones vehicle. It would mean cutting a pound here, an ounce there, looking at every part right down to the smallest screw. It would take a lot of work.

Roos and his men began by completely redesigning the body and chassis, cutting quite a few pounds in the process. They also started looking for the smaller things that could be reduced in weight, going so far as to cut the length of many screws and bolts used in assembly, using smaller fasteners wherever possible, and specifying higher strength, lower weight steel in the frame and some body panels.

Brand new Jeep MAs roll off the assembly line next to brand new Willys American sedans also coming off the line.

The Willys MA regularly showed off its prowess in demonstrations of climbing ability. In this September 1941 photo, probably taken at Willys headquarters in Toledo, Ohio, an MA is parked on the stairs; note its impressive ground clearance.

Roos even weighed the amount of paint used on each vehicle, deciding, according to legend, that one coat would have to do. In the end it did the trick. The redesigned vehicle, now called the Willys MA, had a curb weight of 2,150 pounds. One officer reportedly joked that if some dust had settled on the Willys, it would have put it over the official weight limit.

At this point Willys' production had lagged that of the other two producers, who were then given contracts to build some additional units. In the end Ford built more than 3,500 GP prototypes (the exact number is still debated), Bantam produced 2,674 MK IIs and improved the BRC-40, and Willys built a reported 1,555 MAs, making the Willys prototype the rarest of these early vehicles.

One thing the three vehicles shared, at least among soldiers, was a common designation. It was a "truck, ¼ ton, 4x4." Because just about every wheeled vehicle in the army is considered a General Purpose vehicle, or GP, the GIs nicknamed the little bugs "jeeps," a slurring of the GP initials. But these weren't the first jeeps named by the soldiers. Years earlier there had been a motorized tractor used for hauling guns that was nicknamed a jeep, along with various other trucks and vehicles, including a small

plane. But something happened during testing that ensured that from that point onward there would be only one vehicle that was called a jeep, and it would soon be capitalized as Jeep.

It was in February 1941 when Willys held one of many public demonstrations to show off its little wonder car to a group of reporters. Journalist Katharine Hillyer was driven up and down some extremely steep hills in a Willys MA by veteran Willys test driver "Red" Hausmann. Impressed, and probably a little breathless, Hillyer asked, "What's the name of this thing,

Another Willys MA, also in 1941. Notice the new-style helmets these GIs are wearing.

mister?" Hausmann replied proudly, "It's a Jeep!" Hillyer wrote her story using that name and it was picked up by papers across the land. In little time, "Jeep" came to stand for the 4x4 product produced by Willys-Overland. Some years later, the Jeep name was copyrighted so that no one else could use it.

Testing continued on into summer. Overall, the Willys came out best, and surprisingly, the little Bantam came in second. The Ford, hampered by an underpowered engine, came in last place. Incredibly, though, when it came time to assign contracts for additional vehicles, the Quartermaster Corps said it still preferred the Ford entry. The quartermaster general's reason was once again Ford's proven ability to deliver the goods, versus the questionable financial shape of both Bantam and Willys. The Infantry and Cavalry both protested, and the bidding was thrown open to all three companies.

A contract for 16,000 units of a standardized design was the target now. In this final round Ford bid $782.59 per vehicle, Bantam came in at $788.32 per vehicle, and Willys made the low bid of just $748.74 per vehicle. Despite that low bid—for a superior vehicle no less—the quartermaster again recommended accepting the Ford bid. He protested that Ford was the only builder who could deliver the vehicles on time. At this point, big Bill Knudsen stepped in and refused to accept the Ford bid, saying that in his opinion Willys was a competent source of supply for the vehicles and he was not about to reject the low bid. Since Knudsen, as a former president of GM and a former Ford executive, was considered the world's foremost authority on vehicle production (one of the reasons he was asked to oversee it for the military), the question was settled. The contract went to Willys. The Willys design was modified to incorporate the squared-off front end seen on the Ford, with a slat-type grille. Within days an additional 2,600 Jeeps were added to the Willys order, with production to begin as soon as possible and be completed by January 18, 1942.

Although the big contract was a done deal, both Ford and Bantam continued their efforts to secure Jeep contracts for themselves. In this effort Ford, not surprisingly, was successful while Bantam was not. Because the

The Willys MA evolved into the Willys MB, which was the standard Jeep for World War II and thereafter. Here we see an MB with two men aboard. The driver appears to be Willys vice-president George Ritter; the other man is not identified.

quartermaster already favored Ford, it was fairly easy to convince the military to assign additional contracts to Ford in addition to Willys, so that a second source would be thus secured. Bantam was frozen out of future bids and had to be content with contracts to build trailers for the Jeeps, along with other military hardware. It ended Bantam as a vehicle producer but kept it in business, which was a better deal than it had prior to the Jeep work. Still, it left the Bantam men feeling bitter and betrayed, for they had developed the first vehicle that the others used as a pattern or starting point. As far as the army was concerned, national security was at stake and it could not stop to consider the feelings of a minor automaker, or whether it was fair to force them out of a contract they had worked so hard to win.

Well before the deadline for Willys to complete its big order, there came a development that changed the world forever. On the quiet Sunday morning of December 7, 1941, Japanese warplanes suddenly appeared in the skies above the U.S. naval base at Pearl Harbor, Hawaii. It was early morning and many of the young sailors aboard the line of capital ships swaying with the tide were asleep in their bunks. Whistles began to blow and the sailors ran to their guns to defend the ships. But a battleship resting at berth is generally conceded to be a sitting duck, and that was the case that terrible morning. Wave after wave of Japanese bombers unloaded their

deadly cargoes on the ships below, blasting and destroying as they came on and on. This deadly sneak attack, one of the most cowardly actions in the history of warfare, devastated the U.S. fleet and murdered more than 2,200 American sailors. Despite America's hope that it could remain out of the ongoing conflicts around the world, the country was suddenly dragged into war.

Thankfully the military had had enough foresight to develop the right tool at the right time. Those 18,000-plus Willys Jeeps would be needed immediately, along with hundreds of thousands more. In time, Ford would be given hefty contracts to build tens of thousands of Jeeps that were essentially identical to the Willys design, varying only in minor points. And the little Jeep would prove itself an indispensible tool of war, one of the most important in history, just as Major Lawes predicted. It would be a harsh war, but in the end, the Allies would win, and Japan and Germany would be reduced to ashes, never again to take up arms against another country.

And when the smoke of war had finally cleared, the Jeep was ready for a new role: that of civilian workhorse.

CHAPTER 2

The 1946 Willys was America's first all-steel family station wagon. Painted a deep maroon with wood-look contrasting paint, it mimicked the appearance of expensive wood-bodied station wagons that were the norm back then. It was handsome and practical and could hold up to seven passengers plus cargo.

1946–1963

THE WILLYS-OVERLAND AND WILLYS MOTORS YEARS

IN 1945, WITH THE WAR CLEARLY approaching a close, Willys' management faced a problem it had seen coming for some time already: What would the company produce and sell in the postwar era? The most obvious answer was to go back to building passenger cars, yet that was proving difficult to do. At the time, Willys did not possess the tooling or machinery to produce its own automobile bodies so, like several other independents did, the company purchased complete bodies from body manufacturers like Briggs and Murray. But ever since the Great Depression, the ranks of body builders had shrunk and those that were left had little interest in supplying the needs of a minor company like Willys when the Big Three automakers were standing by ready to take all that they could build.

The debate about what to do had been going on since at least 1943, when there was a sudden change in Willys' management. Joseph Frazer, the well-born and well-liked president of Willys-Overland Motors, was shown the door, replaced as president for a time by board chairman Ward Canaday, who retained that title as well. By 1944, ex-Ford executive Charles "Cast-Iron Charlie" Sorensen had been brought in to serve as president under Chairman Canaday.

By mid 1945, everyone at Willys realized that in order to get into production as quickly as possible, the first postwar product would have to be the little Jeep MB, with a new name plus certain revisions to make it more suitable to peacetime. It would make an excellent farm vehicle, a good service vehicle for garages and gas stations, and an ideal snowplow as well. But management realized that the little Jeep couldn't generate enough sales and profits to keep Willys afloat over the long haul. There had to be other products as well.

DURING THE WAR YEARS, Willys' chief engineer Barney Roos had brought in on retainer a young industrial designer named Brooks Stevens to design a postwar Willys car. Work on the new car had progressed through the various design phases and by 1944 there was a running prototype of an attractive sedan dubbed the Willys 666. It was a bit tall and a bit old-fashioned looking, but it was an improvement over Willys' prewar car and it probably would have done well enough in the postwar sellers market.

Then one day Charles Sorensen called Stevens into his office and told him to set aside the passenger car program. He wanted Stevens to work on something much more important. Sorensen explained, ". . . Willys has no acceptance with any body builder anywhere anymore. Murray, Briggs, Budd—they won't

even talk to us. It is ridiculous for me to even go there because they have no interest in our program whatever. They are too busy working on cars for the big automobile builders. So we have to think of something else."

As one of the top-manufacturing executives in the world, Sorensen knew that automotive-type stamping equipment was not available and would not be for some time. But, ingeniously, he figured he could use stamping presses from the appliance industry as long as the body shapes they would stamp were shallow and not too complex. Turning to Stevens he said, "I want you to develop some vehicles that we can build in a washing machine plant. I'll give you a depth draw of 6 inches. That's it. There is no further press capacity. We can't go to deep drawing shapes for fenders and doors and that sort of thing. What can you develop in this vein?

This delivery truck is a variation of the station wagon body shell. It had steel sides rather than windows and was aimed at florists, package delivery companies, and other businesses that needed a roomy, economical truck.

The 1947 Jeep CJ-2A was a mildly updated version of the wartime Jeep MB. Offering improvements that included better seats, a softer ride, different gear ratios, and more, it proved extremely popular in the postwar era.

We need something that will rub off on our prowess as the builder of Jeeps."

Charged up—he thought at first that he'd been called in to be fired—Stevens rolled up his shirt sleeves and went to work designing a line of vehicles that could be built on a common platform, use many of the same parts, and, most important, share a common look with the wartime Jeep. The importance of the project cannot be overstated; these were the vehicles Willys would be selling for the next 20 years, so he had to get them right.

Before long Stevens had created an entire product lineup consisting of a pickup truck, box truck, station wagon, panel delivery, and a sharp little roadster with a yellow-and-black color scheme. The designs reflected the limitations of the available tooling, with slab sides, square cut fenders, and no complex curves. The look was simple, yet modern and very, very functional. Stevens showed them to Sorensen, who was known

as a man of action "That's it!," cried Sorensen. "Get going full-size," he added, giving Stevens the go-ahead to ready the design for production.

World War II finally ended on August 15, 1945, after the U.S. attacks on Hiroshima and Nagasaki convinced Japan's warlords that their planned suicidal defense of the home islands was futile. As part of America's "Arsenal of Democracy," Willys had produced more than 368,000 Jeep's by war's end. But even before

Several companies created special bodies to fit leftover wartime Jeeps; this wood-bodied station wagon is fairly typical. This was probably done somewhere in Europe.

The 1947 Jeep trucks were very modern-looking for their time and unique in that they offered four-wheel-drive versions at moderate cost in addition to the two-wheel-drive models. They were quite rugged and hardworking vehicles, yet their standard four-cylinder engines also offered great economy.

the actual end of the conflict, Willys was given authorization to get a civilian version of the wartime Jeep into production.

By V-J Day (Victory over Japan) the first of these revised vehicles had come down the assembly line. Called the CJ-2A (for Civilian Jeep model 2, first revision), it was the end result of a development program begun in mid-1944, when a Jeep MB had been pulled off the assembly and sent to the experimental shop, where it was given different gears to make it more suitable for civilian usage, a tailgate, a drawbar, a spare tire mounted on the side of the vehicle, and different springs. Dubbed the CJ-1, it was followed by a small run of vehicles using the name "AGRIJEEP," which was Willys' idea for a product name. Luckily someone within the company realized that such a name would pigeonhole the little Jeep into the agricultural field in buyers' minds. Then came a small run

of CJ-2s, which were further revised and wore brass nameplates that read "JEEP." By the time the final production version of the Jeep, the CJ-2A, was introduced, Willys was calling it the "Universal Jeep," because of its myriad uses.

The civilian Jeep had larger headlights than the wartime Jeep, along with the tailgate, side-mounted spare tire, and all the other improvements seen on the CJ-1 and CJ-2. The seats were more comfortable and, wonder of wonders, the Jeep was offered in several colors as well. The Willys name was stamped into the hood sides.

With a suggested retail price of just $1,090, the new Jeep couldn't help but sell. Willys soon ran into the same problems that every other automotive producer would face in the postwar era, however: a severe shortage of sheet metal, raw materials, and components. Simply put, no automobile manufacturer was able to acquire enough materials to produce anywhere near the volume of vehicles they could sell. Millions of buyers were lined up with cash in their hands ready to buy anything with wheels.

Naturally enough, early buyers of the Jeep CJ-2A were mainly farmers, rural folk, and businesses. Farmers liked the fact that the Jeep could pull a rotary hoe, a plow, or a cultivator, and that its engine and power take-off unit could power a water pump, sawmill, or a rotary auger for drilling wells. The Jeep could haul hay and grain all day and then be used to take the family out to the movies at night. The uses of the new Jeep were truly "Universal."

Not surprisingly, Ford didn't build a civilian version of the Jeep; it really didn't need to since it was already selling all the cars it could build. It probably couldn't have built a Jeep anyway because Willys owned the engine and the wartime rights probably expired as soon as hostilities ceased. Little

Bantam, which had made Jeep trailers during the war, simply faded away, as it was absorbed into another company.

Willys' fiscal year 1945 was profitable despite the end of the war, with net earnings of $2.7 million.

One critical decision Willys management made that year was to continue a prewar effort to maintain and grow its overseas business. To that end, the company reserved 25 percent of its sales volume for overseas markets even though it could have easily sold in America every vehicle it made for the year. Growing a robust overseas business would be vital to Willys' long-term health and set it apart from the other independent producers.

For months Willys produced little other than the CJ-2A. Then in July 1946, the new Brooks Stevens–designed Willys Jeep Station Wagon went into production. It was a landmark vehicle—America's first all-steel family station

The 1947 Willys Jeep station wagons saw little change other than minor mechanical improvements and continued to use the same wood-look paint scheme.

The "Jeep" Station Wagon...Steel Body and Top...Seats for Seven..."Jeep" Engine Economy

wagon. Prior to this station wagon bodies had been carefully made of wood by craftsmen, a very expensive process, and the result was a body that, though it looked great, was costly to build and required annual staining and varnishing to keep in good condition. The high first cost and maintenance headaches had kept station wagons as expensive niche vehicles prior to the advent of the Willys wagon. The new all-steel Willys was easy to build, low in cost, and required little upkeep.

Although Stevens' early sketches and mock-ups depicted the wagon using the same front-end sheet metal as the Universal, over time the design matured and in the end used a larger front clip that, though obviously influenced by the Universal, did not share any sheet metal with it. Stevens cleverly had the wagon body painted with contrasting paint to replicate the expensive "wood-look" of prewar designs to make the new Jeep look handsome and even a bit expensive. There was seating inside for seven people: three in the front seat, three in the back seat, and a seventh person sitting sideways in a single rear seat. With a price tag of $1,495, the new Jeep wagon was a bargain.

Willys-Overland's first full year of strictly peacetime production, 1946, showed mixed results. That year, Willys dealers retailed some 44,464 vehicles[1] in America, of which the majority were CJ-2As. Dollar sales fell by about two-thirds and profits plummeted to just $402,000, but with the first of the new Brooks Stevens–designed Jeep products in production and orders flowing in, things were beginning to improve. Management, however, was in turmoil again; a dissatisfied Ward Canaday kicked Charles Sorensen upstairs to vice chairman, a position with little power, and brought in ex-GM executive James Mooney to serve as president

By 1948 the station wagon could be had in monotone colors and with a six-cylinder engine. The whitewall tires and wraparound bumpers cost extra, and so did the wheel trim rings.

[1] Source: *Automotive News 100-Year Almanac*, April 1996

WILLYS STATION WAGON
6 CYLINDER ENGINE

WHITE SIDEWALL TIRES, GRILLE TRIM AND WRAP-AROUND
BUMPERS OPTIONAL AT ADDITIONAL COST

meet the **Jeepster**

The fleet, low-slung lines of the Jeepster tell you in advance: "Here is a companion for carefree moments".

WILLYS-OVERLAND MOTORS, TOLEDO, OHIO

The Jeepster, a two-wheel-drive sports phaeton, was introduced in 1948. The youthful-looking vehicle was aimed at people who wanted a sporty open car.

Here is the good-looking 1949 Jeep CJ-2A. With a broader choice of colors plus refinements to the mechanical aspects of the tough little vehicle, the CJ-2A appealed to farmers and outdoorsmen.

and chairman. Canaday, one of the company's largest stockholders, was still the power behind the throne. Mooney was under orders to get the passenger car program back on track.

Mooney gave it his best effort. Toward the end of 1946, Willys-Overland released pictures and details of its planned postwar passenger car, the model 6-70, a rather plain two-door sedan wearing 1947 license plates. Although an all-new design, its blatantly prewar styling was not inspiring. No mention was made of when it would be available, but it was to feature an all-new six-cylinder engine of Willys design.

In April 1947 a full line of Jeep Trucks, another of the Brooks Steven's designs, went into production in both ¾-ton and 1-ton versions. Using the same front sheet metal as the wagon, the trucks were available in four body styles: pickup, box truck, stake truck, and canopy. Soon to follow these was the Jeep Delivery. This last, a panel delivery type, was merely a stripped station wagon with flat steel panels where the rear side windows usually went.

The 1947 Jeeps were well-received. The trucks looked modern compared to the older products of International, Studebaker, Ford, Dodge, and

GM, and they offered factory-engineered and installed four-wheel drive, which the others did not. The Jeep station wagons were immensely popular. Willys produced and sold more station wagons that fiscal year than any other maker had ever done in a similar period in history. Management called it a smash success and claimed it ". . . represents our initial post-war invasion of the 'passenger car' field." Meanwhile, CJ-2As continued to sell well both in the United States and in overseas markets. Production of Jeep vehicles increased to 113,602 units for the year. Willys' costs were also rising, however. After the war's end America's labor

Even with a drop in sales for 1949, the Jeep station wagon remained a top-selling wagon and a popular choice for people who needed both a durable work vehicle and a family car.

force decided it deserved more money, and workers had developed strike fever, going out on one strike after another whenever negotiations didn't go their way. At any one time there were dozens of supplier plants on strike, which put a damper on vehicle production. Like many of the smaller automakers, Willys chose to meet union demands for pay increases rather than risk a strike and lose sales. In 1947, a pay increase of 5.5 percent was instituted for hourly workers. To offset the higher costs, vehicle prices were raised 4.5 percent.

During 1947, Willys-Overland invested in raising its production capacity. A new truck cab shop was set up, along with a new panel body

assembly line, new motor assembly line, and a new overhead conveyor for the Jeep CJ line. The forge shop was modernized. With a current capacity of nearly 150,000 bodies per year, the company said it was building toward a goal of being able to produce 300,000 vehicles annually. A new plant in Maywood, California, also was readied for Jeep production that year.

For fiscal year 1947, which ended September 30, the company's income was $138 million and its net profit came to $3.3 million, a solid showing, all things considered. Plans were announced to introduce additional new models in the Jeep lineup to keep the momentum going.

Willys coined a clever slogan to help its vehicles stand apart in the crowded postwar market: "America's Most Useful Vehicles." By 1948 the company had given up the idea of entering the postwar passenger car market with the Willys 6-70 sedan. Instead, during the year management introduced the new Jeepster, a sporty two-door phaeton. The Jeepster used a lot of new tooling for its main body but was based on the Willys station wagon, using its front end sheet metal and most of its mechanical parts as well. It was an odd vehicle to introduce; the phaeton body type had long since gone out of

The new-and-improved CJ-3A for 1949 boasted an undivided windshield and an air vent at the windshield base. It also had a little more legroom, an improved clutch, and window wipers mounted under the windshield rather than on top.

Left: Police departments often purchased Jeeps like this CJ-3A. The little Jeeps were good for parking patrol and waterfront patrolling. For years the local police in the author's hometown—seaside Milford, Connecticut—had a Jeep for beach patrol.

Right: The military version of the CJ-3A was the Willys MC, dubbed the M38 by the military. It offered many improvements over the MB and was rushed into production to meet the demands of the Korean War.

Bottom: For 1950 the senior Jeeps were given a modest restyling. The already-handsome Jeep trucks and wagons got new rounded front fenders, a peaked hood, and a new grille with bright horizontal bars.

style. Buyers now wanted true convertibles when they shopped for an open car, not a soft top that lacked roll-down windows. With a phaeton the only weather protection besides the top were plastic side curtains that snapped into place and often fogged up in cold weather. Besides that, the Jeepster had a four-cylinder engine, and the only other car on the market with a four, besides other Jeeps, was the tiny Crosley mini-car. The fact was, in the postwar market buyers wanted more powerful cars. The Jeepster was so underpowered that the company included overdrive as standard equipment so that it could be driven at reasonable highway

speeds. In its defense, the Jeepster came well-equipped, with overdrive, whitewall tires, full wheel discs, custom interior trim, and two-tone paint—all included in the base price of $1,765. More than 10,000 Jeepsters were built that year.

Also introduced was a new model, the Station Sedan, which used the station wagon body combined with plush—by Jeep standards—interior trim. On the outside it featured monotone paint with cane trim panels that were rather elegant looking. To ensure plenty of power and smoothness, the Station Sedan was equipped with a new Willys six-cylinder engine, a flathead mill displacing 148.5 cubic inches, and 72 horsepower. It was the smallest six in America. Overdrive was also included.

There was even a Jeep Fire Truck catalogued. Based on the CJ-2A, it was ideal for fighting forest fires, or any type of off-road blaze, and was affordable for small towns unable to pay for a regular fore truck. Smaller airports found the little Jeep made an excellent crash truck.

One extremely interesting project during 1948, which would turn out to be a game-changer for Willys, was a request by the federal government for Willys-Overland to build a prototype station wagon with four-wheel drive. This was easy to do since the components that underlay the four-wheel-drive pickup would easily adapt to the station wagon. Once the project was completed, Willys realized it had on its hands a new model for which there would be no competition and that had potential for fairly good sales volume. The company decided to introduce a four-wheel-drive wagon to the retail market in spring 1949.

For fiscal year 1948, Willys-Overland produced 135,528 vehicles, up 19 percent from the prior year, which was a disappointment; there was so much pent-up demand Willys could have sold many thousands more Jeeps if only the materials to build them were readily available. Part of the problem was that Willys also shut down station wagon production for a month during the year when it switched

Left: As part of a program to upgrade and improve the Jeep line, the 1950 senior Jeeps were given a new F-head engine, the four-cylinder Hurricane. Shown here is that engine with its creator, Delmar "Barney" Roos, vice president of engineering at Willys-Overland.

Right: Here is a closer look at the new styling details on the senior Jeep models for 1950. Notice how these minor detail changes made for a much richer looking vehicle. The changes were made midway through the 1950 model year.

The first new postwar military Jeep was the Willys model MC, which the military designated the M38. It was essentially the CJ-3A built to military specifications. It boasted larger headlamps, a one-piece windshield, powerful 24-volt electrical system, and higher ground clearance. Here we see a scene from the little-known Humphrey Bogart film *Battle Circus*, which created the template for the later TV series *M.A.S.H.* That's Keenan Wynne at the wheel of the Jeep, with Bogie as the passenger.

The 1951 Willys Jeep station wagon, equipped with optional wide whitewall tires and chrome wheel rings. Note the subliminal message on the gas pumps: The car is taking 14 gallons while the Jeep takes only 6. How's that for an economy message?

manufacture of wagon bodies to Briggs Manufacturing, which had greater production capacity. The new Jeep plant in Maywood was in operation and built 3,020 Jeeps during the fiscal year, and it was profitable even at that low level of production.

Total sales volume for 1948 was $175 million and a profit of $6.5 million was reported, both good numbers for a small firm like Willys. But up to this point Willys-Overland had been operating in a seller's market where it could command high prices; in 1949, more materials would be available, competition would return to the market, and it was anybody's guess how Willys would do when it went head to head with GM, Ford, and Chrysler.

For 1949, Willys attempted to broaden the appeal of the slow-selling Jeepster by stripping off many of its more desirable standard features and lowering the price. Overdrive, full wheel discs, chrome grille overlay, and a few other items were moved over to the option list, and the Jeepster's retail price dropped to $1,495.

Prices on the rest of the Jeep line were also lowered. The reason: the return of competition in the retail market. Raw materials were in much better supply for 1949 and all of America's vehicle manufacturers were churning out new

cars and trucks as quickly as they could be assembled. Dealers were once again making deals, special sales and discounts returned to the marketplace, and in this atmosphere Willys' management realized they had to cut prices to remain competitive.

Thankfully during the year the federal government ordered some Universals, station wagons, and trucks, as well as spare parts for military Jeeps, which helped sales volume. The company also had a new Jeep Universal to sell as the new Jeep CJ-3A went into production. It looked similar to the CJ-2A but had several important improvements, including a one-piece windshield, better ventilation, and wipers mounted at the base of the windshield rather than at the top. There was a bit more rear seat leg and knee room, a better soft top, an improved clutch, and a much stronger rear axle.

The big product news for 1949 was the July introduction of the Willys Jeep Station Wagon with four-wheel drive. It marked another first for Willys—the first sport utility vehicle (SUV) in the world, combining a family station wagon with the undeniable benefits of four-wheel drive. Willys would have this market all to itself for quite a while, and in time the SUV market would become a gigantic, highly profitable one. But that was in the future.

In the competitive year of 1949 Willys' sales dropped dramatically to $142.3 million, retail unit sales in America were 61,341[2], and profits were $3.4 million. Management explained that the poorer showing was the result of lower vehicle

In 1951, Willys began production of its newest military model, the MD, which the armed forces designated the M38-A1. It offered a potent F-head engine, more room, better ride, more carrying capacity, and several other improvements. Here we see the MD undergoing proving ground testing in Aberdeen, Maryland, the same place where the original Jeep was first tested.

Army test procedures of the day called for rugged driving and basically punishing the vehicle until something broke or until the driver was worn out. Here we see an MD/M38-A1 with all four wheels off the ground.

[2] Source: *Automotive News 100-Year Almanac*, April 1996

The visual differences between the M38 (left) and M38-A1 (right) are clearly illustrated in this photo. Both were tough vehicles, but the M38-A1 boasted many improvements, including lower weight and higher ground clearance.

The M38-A1 was later fitted with the Recoilless Rifle and was an aggressive and highly maneuverable tank destroyer.

end of the fiscal year, Willys still had about $15 million in government orders to fill, not a lot but at least they had some sort of backlog to boast of. Production at the California plant was rising. It produced 5,295 Jeeps for the year and remained profitable. Meanwhile, the near constant turmoil in the executive ranks continued, with chairman and president Mooney given the heave-ho as Ward Canaday once more took over the reins at Willys-Overland.

So Willys entered 1950 with a small order backlog, a new Universal model, and a serious competitive environment. There were no new models or much that was new in existing models during the first half of the model year, and sales were slow as a result. The company had continued to build small quantities of the CJ-2A as it ramped up production of its replacement, but before long the CJ-3A was the sole Universal. Then on March 30, 1950, some relief came for Willys' beleaguered dealers; the company unveiled new models of the senior vehicle line.

Externally the new senior Jeeps—the Station Wagon, Jeepster, Truck, and Panel Delivery— looked similar, though the styling changes made

pricing, as well as a new policy allowing dealers to stock fewer vehicles. This last move meant that many dealers sold down their inventory without reordering as many replacement vehicles, which sharply cut Willys production. But steps were taken to reduce overhead, particularly in administration, and a new $6 million stamping plant was coming on-line that would lower the cost of producing bodies. Thankfully, at the

them more handsome by modernizing their appearance. Front fenders now were rounded, with the front edges coming to a graceful peak. Likewise, the rounded hood front also featured a peaked nose. The grille area now bowed outward in a V-shape, and horizontal chrome bars gave the front end a much richer look.

Equally big was the change under the hood. The standard engine now was a greatly revised version of the Go-Devil. Dubbed the Hurricane, this lusty four-cylinder engine had a novel F-head design in which the intake valves were moved to the head while the exhaust valves remained in the block. This provided for larger intake valves and better breathing. Because of this, the Hurricane four-cylinder delivered 72 horsepower, a large increase over the former engine and, coincidentally, the same power output as the Willys Lightening Six. That situation would have confused customers, so the flathead Six was given an increase in displacement to 161 cid and now produced 75 horsepower. To give the retail network a boost, the company hosted a large gathering on March 3, 1950, to announce and show off the new models.

The civilian products were not the only new models for 1950. With war ready to flare up at any moment on the Korean Peninsula, the

U.S. Army asked Willys to design a new, better military Jeep and rush it into production. The result was what Willys called the MC, a logical progression from the models MA and MB. It shared many of the improvements seen in the CJ-3A and looked similar as well. The army dubbed it the M38. It had larger headlights, a one-piece windshield, 24-volt electrical system, and higher ground clearance. Other improvements included a stronger frame, beefier transmission and transfer case, electric windshield wipers, and heavier-duty springs. The expected war in Korea broke out in June 1950, and by the end of the year, Willys had more than $100 million in backorders with the military, an extraordinary success for the company.

But 1950 proved a challenging year for Willys-Overland. During the first six months of the fiscal year, before the improved models were introduced, sales were in the basement and the company lost nearly a million dollars. Then, in the second half of the year, the new models were available and sales grew 97 percent over the first half—some 23 percent over the similar period in 1949—and the company earned more than $2.5 million, leaving a net profit for the year of $1.6 million.

Bright spots for 1950 included that huge government order backlog, along with the

Here's another look at the 1951 Willys station wagon. In this view the car has its standard black tires and no trim rings, and it still looks handsome.

Anyone looking for more luxury in a Willys wagon could order the Deluxe station wagon, which featured cane-work trim like the earlier Station Sedan, along with a nicer interior, chrome strip on the hood sides, and other luxury touches.

The new CJ for 1953 was the CJ-3B, or "high-hood" Jeep. It offered a standard 72-horsepower Hurricane F-head four-cylinder engine for improved acceleration and pulling power. This was a taller engine than the wartime Go-Devil, necessitating the higher hood.

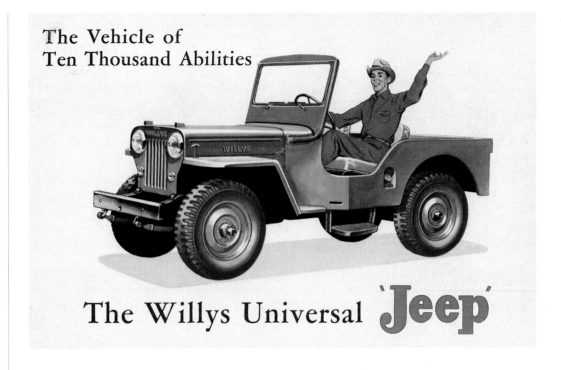

The Vehicle of Ten Thousand Abilities

The Willys Universal `Jeep`

Here's a side view of the new CJ-3B, in which you can better see the higher hood line needed to accommodate the F-Head Hurricane engine.

production of the 250,000th civilian Universal Jeep and the shipment of the 100,000th Universal Jeep for export. The company's station wagon remained the top-selling wagon in the country, and the top-selling station wagon in the export market as well. One exciting event

was a large contract to supply automaker Kaiser-Frazer Corporation with four- and six-cylinder engines for its upcoming small car called the Henry J. The deal called for thousands of these engines and would greatly enhance Willys-Overland's bottom line.

Most important, the company once again had momentum in the marketplace. With revised products, new engines, and a strong backlog of orders, Willys-Overland entered the 1951 fiscal year brimming with well-earned confidence.

The company had a new engineer on staff. Clyde Paton was given that appointment on July 24. This relatively minor event is notable only because Paton was one of the better automotive engineers in the country and he had been pitching an idea for a smaller car to any company that would give him an audience. Several had, though eventually all turned him down. But sometime after he spoke to Ward Canaday, he was given a job with the company. Apparently Canaday's dream of

producing a postwar Willys passenger car still burned brightly.

Jeep sales continued to turn upward in 1951, as public acceptance of the freshened Jeep lineup was matched by the military's urgent need for new military Jeeps as well as replacement parts for the rapidly aging World War II–era Jeep MBs in use. There were still many thousands of these in service and they were beginning to need more frequent repair due to their age and hard use.

New products for 1951 included versions of the civilian Jeep dubbed the Farm Jeep and the Jeep Tractor. The Farm Jeep was a civilian Jeep with a factory-installed hydraulic lift for use with various farming attachments, plus a drawbar, heavy-duty suspension, and an engine governor. The Jeep Tractor was designed strictly for off-road use and came with a factory-installed hydraulic lift, power take-off, a governor, drawbar, heavy-duty suspension, front bumper weight, propeller shaft guards, and a radiator screen. It lacked front shocks, spare tire, windshield, tailgate, lights, speedometer assembly, and horn—the things a road-going vehicle would use. Neither of these products found wide acceptance and

they were eventually discontinued after small numbers were built.

Willys' engineering department, clothed in secrecy, worked overtime that year. Besides their ordinary duties, the engineers were hard at work on another new military Jeep, preliminary work on a new civilian Jeep, and at long last, a true postwar passenger car.

During 1951 the company noted that in addition to being a fairly large vehicle producer and engine supplier, it was also the third largest producer of aluminum forgings in America and was supplying these to military aircraft manufacturers. It was also an important supplier of steel forgings.

To say that 1951 was a good year for the corporation would be an understatement; it was a tremendous year. Sales volume more than doubled, to $219,861,553 and profits of $4.58 million were recorded. Dollar volume was divided about equally between civilian and military sales and the company was ranked among the 25 largest producers of military equipment. What came as a surprise to many was the backlog of orders at year's end—a whopping $250 million, a greater amount than that year's sales volume.

Left: Near the end of 1954, Willys Motors introduced the civilian version of the M38-A1, dubbed the CJ-5. It was larger and more stylish than the earlier CJs and would become a legend. Production of the CJ-5 ran longer than any other CJ vehicle.

Right: The 1955 CJ-5: Note the sharp red paint, matching wheels, and stylish gray interior trim. Although the CJ-5 became the most popular CJ, the CJ-3B remained in production due to its continuing popularity and lower price.

The 1956 Willys Jeep station wagons had a slight appearance change. The middle grille bar was raised and a neat two-tone paint scheme was offered.

Willys also announced that it would soon introduce its new car, the Aero Willys, a two-door sedan with good looks, the same sturdy engines as the Jeeps, and solid engineering courtesy of Clyde Paton. Scheduled to be introduced in January 1952, it would take Willys firmly into the now fully competitive automobile market. Canaday was at last getting the passenger car he'd wanted since 1946, though the market had changed drastically since that time.

When the 1952 model year opened, the Jeep lineup was missing two-wheel-drive trucks; over the prior two years their sales had slipped to where it was hardly worth building them, while the four-wheel-drive trucks were selling well. The decision to drop the two-wheelers made sense from an economic standpoint, but it was sad to see the company exit the regular pickup market. Also dropped was the Jeepster, and this was simply because it had never sold as Willys management had hoped. Because so much of Willys' production now was going to the military, the company couldn't produce all the civilian Jeeps it wanted to, so it concentrated on the more profitable ones. With the new Aero passenger car, there was little need for the Jeepster anyway.

The newest member of the Jeep family of hard-working vehicles was this small DJ-3A, which was a two-wheel-drive version of the earlier CJ-3A. This smart little car was available as an open roadster, convertible, or with a steel hardtop with fiberglass roof panel. These became popular as delivery vehicles for pharmacies and flower shops.

Down on the farm, the Jeep CJ-5 (a 1956 model is shown here) was greatly admired for its usefulness. It could carry tools and materials, power farm machinery, and later be used to drive the family into town at the end of a workday.

As usual, Willys was also hampered by insufficient working capital, which limited its ability to produce as many vehicles as it could have sold. And that working capital was further reduced by the demands of launching the new passenger cars. The end result of all this was that Willys' dealers couldn't get enough vehicles for stock purposes and had to sell on the basis of delivery in 30 to 60 days on any civilian four-wheel-drive vehicle. That certainly put a damper on retail sales.

The company announced the newest military Jeep toward the end of 1951, so for fiscal 1952 the majority of military Jeeps being produced

were the new M-38A1 models, which, being the company's fourth military model, Willys designated the MD. The M-38A1 was quite an improvement over the wartime Jeep and even the M-38. The new Jeep was powered by the potent F-head engine, so its performance was much improved, and the vehicle was slightly larger, had a better ride, was more comfortable, and even weighed a bit less than the M-38. Over time, more than 100,000 of these tough little Jeeps would be built. Little did the company know that this would be the last volume-selling military Jeep it would produce.

Because so much emphasis was being put on the new Willys Aero car, there was little change in the remaining Jeep lineup. Station wagons got a new optional engine dubbed the Hurricane Six, an F-head version of the Lightning Six that produced 90 horsepower, a nice 20 percent upgrade from the former's 75 horsepower. Wagons also got stylish new wraparound read bumpers. Advertising efforts were redoubled; Willys became the first sponsor for the new television variety show *Omnibus*, hosted by the debonair Alistair Cooke.

Willys was expanding in the overseas markets. Jeep vehicles were now being produced

The export business was always important for Willys, and it grew in importance as the years went by. The company shipped fully built-up vehicles, as well as kits of parts that were then assembled overseas for local markets. This appears to be a crate of unassembled parts. Note the stencil being used to paint the Jeep logo onto the box.

in Belgium, the Netherlands, Denmark, India, Ireland, South Africa, Indonesia, Mexico, and Australia, with more countries to follow.

Regardless of the lack of major changes, Willys was on a roll and reported an all-time sales record of $301 million for 1952, a 37 percent increase from 1951. Net profits of $6 million were recorded. During the fiscal year 1952, Willys produced more than 148,000 vehicles, of which military Jeeps accounted for more than 47,500 units. This compared to approximately 25,200 military Jeeps built in 1951, so nearly all of Willys' increase had come from military orders. Also noted was that Willys was the fifth largest vehicle producer in the United States, rising to that position from being ninth in 1950 and seventh in 1951. The company was in third place in export shipments of commercial vehicles and had 2,300 distributors and dealers in foreign countries.

During the year, the 1,000,000th Jeep was produced. Even though Willys production was stepped up to meet demand, at year-end the company still had an order backlog valued at $225 million. It was another great year for Willys-Overland Motors.

It was expected that 1953 would be Willys' biggest year yet. The company was celebrating its 50th anniversary, dating back to being the automotive division of the Standard Wheel

Company in 1903. New Aero Willys four-door sedans were being introduced for 1953, along with a new four-wheel-drive Sedan Delivery wagon and the new CJ-3B civilian Jeep. This last model was the company's response to appeals for more power in the little Jeep. Since the only engine that could fit under a Jeep's hood was a four-cylinder, Willys was limited to either the flathead engine it was using—which everyone felt was underpowered—or the F-head Hurricane Four used in the wagons and trucks. But the F-head was a tall engine, and in order to fit it under the hood of the CJ, the hood had to be raised, along with the cowl and grille, of course, and various mechanical changes had to be introduced to make it all possible. The result was called the CJ-3B (also known as the "high hood Jeep"), which had a different face, classic flat fenders, and greater commercial appeal. In time, the CJ-3B would gain a large following. That year the CJ-3A went out of production.

As always, Willys' engineers and product planners were working on new products and variations of existing products in an effort to build sales volume. One new vehicle was the experimental Aero Jeep, a lightweight (1,400 pounds) vehicle designed for airborne

operations. The company also received a contract to work on a low-cost platform vehicle for hauling supplies. In addition, some specialized Jeep postal vehicles went into service. These included four-wheel-drive Universals with steel hardtops and a fleet of two-wheel-drive Sedan Deliveries.

On Lincoln's Birthday, February 12, 1953, Willys-Overland Motors celebrated its 50th year in business. It was a joyous occasion, though short-lived. Two months later, Ward Canaday sold the operating assets of the company, essentially all of its business, to the Kaiser Manufacturing Company, a subsidiary of automaker Kaiser Motors Corporation (formerly named Kaiser-Frazer Corporation), which planned to merge the two operations. Needless to say, it came as a shock. Although business pundits had been extolling the benefits of the independent automakers merging, the Willys-Kaiser combination was the first, and no one had seen it coming. It was not actually a merger. The Kaiser interests bought only the operating assets of Willys-Overland, not

During 1957 the company produced the Mechanical Mule, a small platform carrier-type vehicle, for the military. It could be driven as shown, or a soldier could walk alongside it to allow more cargo on board.

The 1957 FC-150 was a very compact truck, built on a short 81-inch wheelbase. But it was built tough, and with its rugged Jeep four-wheel drive, it could haul loads where other trucks couldn't.

the company itself. The corporation survived for a time as a holding company for Ward Canaday and friends. The new company, considered a subsidiary of Kaiser Motors, was immediately renamed Willys Motors Inc.

The sole reason for joining Kaiser and Willys operations was that Kaiser-Frazer Corporation was failing, going down quickly, and its chairman Henry J. Kaiser was desperately trying to salvage his company. As Kaiser automobile sales fell, he looked about for another automotive company to team up with, one that could potentially save his own firm. The only one that made sense to him was Willys-Overland. Willys was small, but it was selling more vehicles than Kaiser was, and it was a solidly profitable company with essentially no competition in the four-wheel-drive market and none on the horizon. In addition, Willys chairman Ward Canaday was ready to cash in on his investment in Willys and would agree to sell if the price was right. Henry Kaiser figured he could join his firm with Willys and then use the latter's profits to offset Kaiser losses for a time, until the problems could be fixed or—if need be—the Kaiser automotive part were wound down. In either event, the profitable Willys operation would still be around, and thousands of Kaiser stockholders would own shares in a profitable company and wouldn't see their investments wiped out. The total cost of buying Willys' $76 million in assets was $60.8 million, of which some $32 million was paid in cash.

Unfortunately, all this had a negative effect on the business itself. In a retail market that was up significantly in 1953, Willys Motors sales fell slightly and thus its market share also fell. At the same time, Kaiser automobile sales utterly collapsed.

At year end, the new company reported its consolidated results in its annual report to stockholders. Because of the absolute disintegration of Kaiser auto sales and the high cost of melding the two company's operations,

Another interesting vehicle that Jeep engineers created was this XM443, a platform vehicle significantly larger and more powerful than the Mechanical Mule. The XM443 could carry large cargos or up to six troops. It could be fitted with a weather enclosure and driven on the highway. Sadly, it never got beyond the testing stage.

"Maverick Special" **Jeep** Station Wagon

Meet America's most distinguished vehicle—a "Maverick Special" 'Jeep' Station Wagon! Here is prime performance at a price no other station wagon can touch. This is the station wagon with a built-in budget —costs less to buy, less to own and operate yet has higher resale value. Ideal as a family car or a second car, the 'Jeep' Station Wagon combines rugged utility with modern styling and convenience. It is powered by the world famous 'Jeep' 4 cylinder High Torque Hurricane engine; has a new spring suspension system, fashionable new interior and trim, 1-piece windshield, and that smart low look—stands only 70½" high.

COCHRAN & CELLI
'Jeep' Division
12TH & HARRISON
OAKLAND HI 4-0055

total sales of Kaiser Motors Corporation and Willys Motors Inc. came to just $365,666,229. Of this total, Willys' share was $290.7 million and the subsidiary reported a profit of $1.6 million, both down from the prior year. But when combined with the huge losses at the Kaiser operation, the net result was a loss of $27 million for the year. Kaiser's operating loss can only be estimated but must have been close to $35 million, a staggering amount for a company of that size in that decade. Obviously Mr. Kaiser

made his move at the right moment. His firm had been on the verge of going under.

Operations and manufacturing were consolidated mainly at Willys' facilities in Toledo, Ohio. This would cut costs while allowing Kaiser to sell its huge plant in Willow Run, Michigan. From that point on, Kaiser automobiles would be assembled in the Willys plant. It was hoped that consolidation would bring profitability back to the company, but that was not to be. Unbeknownst to them, Willys and Kaiser were heading into the most competitive period in the history of the American automobile industry. From late 1953 to late 1954, Ford and Chevrolet would stage an epic battle for supremacy in the automobile market and as a result would nearly destroy the few remaining American independent automakers: Nash, Hudson, Packard, Studebaker, and Kaiser and Willys. It would be all the company could do simply to hang on.

During the fall of 1954, the new F-head–powered Universal CJ-5 entered production.

Willys Motors was the proud sponsor of the popular TV series *Maverick*, which made a star out of James Garner. To play off of its renown, Willys introduced the Maverick Special two-wheel-drive station wagon for family use. With special two-tone paint and chrome side moldings, the Maverick Special also boasted upgraded interior trim and a low, low price of just $1,895.

During 1957, Willys supplied Jeeps to Fairmont Railway Motors of Fairmont, Minnesota, which converted them into Hy-Rail units that could be driven on railroad tracks. Used by track supervisors, track patrolmen, line repairmen, and others, the vehicles' railroad wheels swung up for driving on regular roads.

The CJ-5 for 1958 continued to attract buyers who were looking for a workhorse vehicle with durability and the go-anywhere capability.

The CJ-5 was the civilian version of the M38-A1 military Jeep. It was more stylish than the earlier civilian Jeeps, rode an 81-inch wheelbase, and boasted 4 more square feet of interior space, for improved passenger room and greater cargo-carrying ability. The vehicle's ride quality was also improved. The new CJ-5 would become a legend, a worldwide symbol of Jeep, in the years to come.

In 1954, Willys began to offer the Kaiser 226-cid six-cylinder engine, dubbed the Super Hurricane, in the four-wheel-drive station wagons and pickups. Pumping out a generous 115 horsepower, it transformed the senior Jeeps into much better all-around vehicles, with improved acceleration and greater smoothness. The senior line got revised grilles, with three crossbars rather than five, giving the front a cleaner look. Marketing people also changed the names of several models. The Jeep station wagon was now called

the Utility Wagon, the delivery truck was now the Utility Delivery, and the pickup became the Utility Pickup. New specialized vehicles included an open Personnel Carrier based on the station wagon, and a four-wheel-drive ambulance, also based on the wagon.

Export sales set a new record in 1954, with more than 45,000 vehicles shipped to foreign markets. A new subsidiary was formed called Willys-Overland do Brasil, to build Jeep vehicles for the local market. Surprisingly, this branch would grow to become one of the largest automakers in South America, with production rivaling Jeep in America.

But in the extraordinarily tough U.S. market, it was another bad year for Kaiser-Willys (as it often referred to itself), even worse than 1953. The combined company lost $35.4 million.

As the 1955 fiscal year opened, Willys sales were beginning to climb and the company

of the largest automakers in South America. In fact, for years the two firms were the top automakers in the South American market.

The new CJ-5 got off to a good start, aided by an effective advertising program and the products' obvious superiority. The Aero Willys car, on the other hand, suffered a terrible slowdown in sales, a trend that began in the competitive 1954 model year. The company added more specialty vehicles to its portfolio as it reluctantly eased its way out of the passenger car market. By year end, U.S. production of both Willys and Kaiser cars had been discontinued.

For the 1955 fiscal year, total sales volume fell like a stone to $167 million of which $161 million was attributed to Willys, the rest to Kaiser. Amazingly, the company reported a net profit of $5 million. Because of tax-loss carry-forwards dating back to Kaiser-Frazer, this income was tax-free.

When 1956 opened, the Kaiser interests were restructuring their various companies.

revealed that it had earned a profit in the first quarter. It also announced creation of another new subsidiary, Industrias Kaiser Argentina, to build Jeep Universals, wagons, and pickups for the Argentinean market, along with the Kaiser passenger car. Like Willys do Brasil, this company would also eventually become one

Here's a good view of the handsome Forward Control FC-170 heavy-duty truck. Its natural element was off-road, where its traction and durability could best be put to use.

The CJ-6 for 1959. The long-wheelbase Jeep CJ-6 debuted in 1956 and quickly became a popular vehicle overseas, where it was often used as a small pickup truck. It was also useful here in the United States because its longer body provided much more carrying room for supplies and equipment.

Kaiser Motors changed its name to Kaiser Industries Corporation and acquired all the stock of the Henry J. Kaiser Company. Kaiser Industries thus became a major factor in the worldwide engineering and construction business, steel production, aluminum and chemical manufacturing, cement and other products, along with owning Willys Motors. But the greatest benefit of this consolidation was the ability to use the Kaiser Motors (née Kaiser-Frazer) tax-loss carry-forwards to their greatest extent. The company earned nearly $15 million that year, and all of it was tax free.

No military Jeeps were produced during 1956. The company did complete about $24 million in defense and government orders, mainly replacement parts for the existing fleet. A new civilian Jeep series called the DJ-3A Dispatcher debuted. It was essentially the old CJ-3A body on a simplified two-wheel-drive chassis. Designed to be an inexpensive delivery car or personal fun car, prices began at a mere

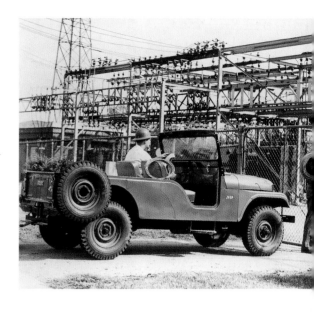

$1,205 for a stripped open roadster with no top. Other models included a convertible and a steel cab hardtop with a fiberglass roof panel. Also introduced was the new four-wheel-drive CJ-6 model. Based on the CJ-5, it had a 20-inch longer wheelbase, making it more suited for

During 1959, Willys Motors received orders for the military version of the CJ-6, which was dubbed the M-170. A forward lines ambulance, these were vitally important to the military and helped save many lives.

In 1959, the company introduced the new Jeep Surrey, a two-wheel-drive DJ-3A dressed up in loud colors and equipped with striped seats and a striped, fringed top. Three colors were offered: green, blue, and pink, with the latter being the most popular. Many resort hotels bought these fun little vehicles.

carrying cargo and equipment. It proved very popular in overseas markets. Since 1953, Willys export sales had exceeded its domestic sales volume and this was true again in 1956.

Willys introduced two interesting new trucks for 1957, the four-cylinder 81-inch wheelbase FC-150 Forward Control pickup and the longer 103.5-inch wheelbase six-cylinder FC-170. The two trucks sported unusual styling, which one magazine called the "helicopter look" because of its "forward cab" design. The two trucks were another Willys attempt to expand its market share. The FC-150 had a 5,000-pound GVW, while the FC-170 had a 7,000-pound GVW. Neither truck sold as well as was hoped for, probably because the styling was simply too unusual for mainstream buyers to accept in that very conservative era. Specialty vehicles, including airport ground service trucks, were also introduced in 1957, along with tow trucks and special railroad trucks that could ride the rails bringing track crews to various work sites.

Sales by Willys Motors in 1957 totaled just $140 million, and a net profit of $5 million was reported. Once again, there was no tax due that year. From 1955 to 1957, Kaiser Industries paid no federal income tax because of its tax-loss carry-forwards, meaning the company had acquired Willys at very little cost. But Willys' low profitability was affecting its new product budget.

It could be seen during the 1958–1962 period when the company didn't introduce any really significant new models, just variations of existing products. Sales in 1958 were $136 million, and the company earned $6.8 million. Willys Overland do Brasil announced a program to increase its production capacity to 60,000 units annually. U.S. retail sales for 1959 were up significantly, the result of efforts by general manager of sales Cruse Moss. He was determined to improve Willys' retail efforts. Amazingly, Moss was able to shake the Willys dealer network out of its lethargy, and sales showed a marked improvement every

In 1959, Jeep contract stylist Brooks Stevens created this special Jeep Harlequin show car with unique wheel covers, special paint, and a luxurious interior. Where this vehicle is today is unknown.

Here is a 1960 two-wheel-drive DJ-3A convertible. Willys pitched the convertible as a fun roadster, a sort of pseudo-sports car, but it's doubtful many were purchased for that reason. Instead, the DJ-3A market seemed to be light, low-cost delivery for small companies.

month. The 1959 fiscal year sales totaled $153.8 million and a profit of $10.6 million was reported. The company also delivered to the army several prototypes of a new platform vehicle dubbed the XM 443, designed to carry 3/4 ton of cargo or up to six soldiers. By year end, Willys vehicles were being assembled in 22 countries around the world.

Momentum continued into 1960 with sales climbing to $157 million and a $9.2 million profit recorded. Domestic unit sales of 31,940 units were a new high for Willys Motors and its 1,425 U.S. dealers, as were royalty and dividend income from overseas operations. Overseas unit sales came to 28,600. In the Jeep product line, the Maverick name was dropped from the two-wheel-drive family wagon, though the vehicle itself remained in the lineup with revised and very attractive new side moldings and two-tone paint.

In that same year, Willys-Overland do Brasil sold a whopping 38,500 vehicles, while IKA sold 32,900—both more than the U.S. operation did. But because Willys Motors was only part owner of the two firms, their sales were not included in its own totals, only royalties and dividends earned. During the year, Cruse Moss was named vice president of sales, recognition of the outstanding work he'd done getting the retail operation moving forward.

In an effort to expand its government business, which shrank tremendously when the army switched to buying a Ford-built

'Jeep' *Fleetvan*

In 1961, the Jeep Fleetvans were unveiled. The FJ-3 was a short-bodied delivery truck sold to the U.S. Post Office. The FJ-3A shown here had a longer wheelbase and much longer body and was sold to small businesses as a delivery van. Willys Motors built the chassis; the body was produce by Highway Products of Ohio.

four-wheel-drive tactical vehicle called the M-151 Mutt, Willys introduced a new sit-stand delivery vehicle called the FJ-3 Fleetvan and won a contract to produce 6,025 of them for the U.S. Post Office. Willys built only the chassis for these vehicles; the body came from Highway Products, an Ohio-based body builder.

Alarmingly, a competitor made its first appearance toward the end of 1960. The all-new 1961 Scout from International Harvester was a short wheelbase two- or four-wheel-drive vehicle that offered much better creature comfort and roominess than the Jeep CJ-5, as well as a range of models, including roadster, pickup or wagon, along with a variety of soft and hardtops. This

was the first real competition Jeep had to face and it was a tough one.

In 1961, Willys' sales dropped in line with the rest of the industry, due to an economic slowdown that hit the automobile business particularly hard. The slowdown was short-lived, and by year end sales were on the rise again. But for the fiscal year, Willys' profit fell to $7.2 million. Highlights for the year included completing an order for 4,000 CJ-3Bs for the Turkish Army. These vehicles were assembled in Turkey by Turk Willys-Overland. Other news included an order from the U.S. Army for M170 frontline ambulances. Also in 1961, a new version of the Fleetvan debuted. Called the FJ-3A, it had a longer, larger body for carrying more cargo. It was offered on the retail market, where it enjoyed modest sales. The Forward Control line added three new 1-ton dual rear-wheel models: pickup, stake, and cab and chassis.

For 1962, the Willys station wagons were renamed Jeep Travelers and new paint schemes were introduced to freshen the aging vehicles. The company invested heavily in a new six-cylinder engine, the first overhead-cam engine by a major American producer. With 230 cubic inches, it produced a healthy 140 horsepower and 210 lb-ft of torque. Good news came on the government vehicles front: Underbidding Ford, Willys won the contract to build the M-151 Mutt tactical truck. The new contract called for 18,625 units.

Willys reported record sales for 1962 based mostly on the introduction of a completely new line of Jeep wagons and pickups that supercharged unit sales in the fourth quarter. However, though sales were up, the cost of tooling for the new vehicles was quite large by

Willys standards—an estimated $12 million—so for the year the company reported a loss of $469,000.

The new vehicles were the Wagoneer and the Gladiator—the first, a groundbreaking new station wagon that would go on to become legendary, the latter a handsome brute of a pickup truck that would bring Jeep into direct competition with the Big Three makers, as well as competitor International Harvester.

First the Wagoneer. To call it revolutionary is more than apt; it was the first four-door four-wheel-drive family wagon, the first to offer independent front suspension, the first to combine an optional automatic transmission with four-wheel drive. Available in both two- and four-wheel-drive versions, as well as two- and four-door models, Wagoneer came with the new OHC six-cylinder engine, a manual three-speed transmission, or with optional overdrive, four-speed manual and automatic transmission choices. It boasted an outstanding

Here is the Willys jeep station wagon for 1962. This year the wagon could be ordered with the new overhead cam Super Hurricane six-cylinder engine for greater power and smoothness.

design by Jim Angers, head of Willys Styling department, and the look was bold and utterly original. The Wagoneer's styling was car-like but larger. Though compact in dimensions (it rode a 110-inch wheelbase), it was extremely roomy and looked much larger than it was. It set the tone and the standard for every sports utility vehicle that followed it, right to the present time. It was simply a complete game-changer for the industry, though few realized it at the time.

The Gladiator pickup shared most of the revolutionary engineering of the Wagoneer and also shared the same front end sheet metal, though with larger flaring on the fenders. It was offered in two series, J-200 and J-300, in a wide variety of models, including both two- and four-wheel-drive versions, and ½-ton,

¾-ton, and 1-ton models, with a choice of a Thriftside or Townside body, Platform Stake body, or as a cab and chassis. It also offered two wheelbases: 120-inch and 126-inch, to handle a 7- or 8-foot bed, and a range of GVW (gross vehicle weight) ratings up to 8,600 pounds. Power steering and power brakes were now available. There was also a large new panel truck, based on the two-door Wagoneer body but with sheet metal rather than window sides.

Because of the cost and complexity of introducing the new Wagoneer and Gladiator, the rest of the product line was essentially carryover. The focus would be on the hot new products for 1963.

Sales were robust, and before long, dealers found themselves in short supply and hollering for more production. But Jeep had underestimated

The biggest Jeep news in years was the late 1962 introduction of the all-new 1963 Jeep Wagoneer, which would eventually replace the Willys station wagon. It offered four doors (or two), automatic transmission, and the powerful OHC six introduced in early 1962. This revolutionary SUV would remain in production through 1991.

Here is the all-new 1963 Jeep Gladiator truck, sporting the less-expensive Thriftside pickup box. These smart, attractive trucks could be ordered with either two- or four-wheel drive and offered a long list of optional extras.

the strong reaction from the public, and although they set fairly high production goals, they couldn't build enough Wagoneers and Gladiators to meet demand. Even so, many months saw new sales records set regardless.

Jeep sales and profits rose strongly for 1963, with dollar volume of $220 million and an operating profit of $9.3 million before interest and taxes. New U.S. records were set for the year for retail sales as well as wholesale shipments. Government sales were up strongly as well,

thanks to the delivery of 8,204 M151 Mutts. On a down note, Jeep lost the latest bidding for the M-151 contract, and 1964 would be the last year the company would produce that vehicle for some time.

There was sad news. In March 1963, Willys Motors president Steve Girard announced that the board of directors had voted to change the name of the company to Kaiser Jeep Corporation, laying the grand old Willys name into the grave of automotive memories. The reason given was "to properly identify the Toledo company as one of the growing Kaiser family of industries." In other words, to stroke Henry J.'s ego. It was a sad and sudden passing.

The newly named company was flexing its muscles, ready to expand its base both in the retail arena and the critical military market. The next few years would see Jeep expand into new markets as it fought to solidify its market share in the face of new competition from the major producers. How it would end up was anyone's guess.

CHAPTER 3

The new glamour star for 1964 was the Jeep Universal Tuxedo Park. This was a separate model in the CJ-5 and CJ-6 series, not an option package, and was an attempt to give the little Jeep a tad more flash and style. Notice the chrome mirror, hood hinges, and bumper. The color-coordinated interior trim and top, along with the whitewall tires and full-wheel discs, really dress up this CJ-5.

1964–1969

MR. KAISER'S JEEP

AS GOOD AS 1963 HAD BEEN, 1964 WAS AN EVEN BETTER YEAR FOR JEEP. After the Studebaker Corporation announced at the end of 1963 that it would cease manufacturing cars and trucks in the United States, Kaiser Jeep executives purchased one of the larger Studebaker factories in South Bend, Indiana, and took over the contract to build 5-ton army trucks. This move launched Jeep into the heavy-duty military truck market and was the beginning of a strong new emphasis on government business. Export volume climbed 22 percent for the year as well. Over in India, Mahindra and Mahindra, Jeep builders for the local market, were undertaking a major expansion program that would make them one of the largest Jeep manufacturers in the world. By year's end, they purchased the tooling to make the Forward Control models, moved it to India, and began producing the unique trucks there for the local market. They would keep the FC in production into the 1990s.

There was a lot of exciting product news. During the year, Kaiser Jeep introduced its first attempt at a luxuriously upgraded Universal with the announcement of two sporty new models: the CJ-5A Tuxedo Park Mark IV and the CJ-6A Tuxedo Park Mark IV. Both of these vehicles were standard CJs with added special features that included chromed mirrors, hood latches, bumpers, windshield hinges, and gas cap. Inside was a brightly colored interior trim to coordinate with the cheerful exterior colors, of which four were offered: white, blue, green, and red. There were also color-coordinated vinyl soft tops and spare tire covers, and whitewall tires and full chrome wheel discs were available. The Tuxedo Park models were very dressy for the time and initial response was good.

WAGONEER AND GLADIATOR returned with almost no change in appearance but now offered factory air conditioning, an idea almost unheard of for a truck-type station wagon. It arrived because Jeep's customers were asking for it. They considered the Wagoneer a passenger car replacement, not a work vehicle, and they wanted the sort of comfort and convenience features found in regular passenger cars. Those same customers were also asking for more engine power, and Jeep had something in the works for them, though it wouldn't debut until mid-1965.

Retail sales grew 5.6 percent for the year, while total dollar volume jumped to $255.5 million. This big increase was due mainly to a large jump in military orders. Government sales volume was up some $23 million for the year, though it was only moderately profitable.

Top: Virginia Moss, wife of Kaiser Jeep executive Cruse Moss, poses with one of the Jeep Wagoneer Courtesy Cars used at the New York World's Fair. The lovely Mrs. Moss, nee Virginia Patton, appeared in the holiday movie classic *It's a Wonderful Life* as George Bailey's sister-in-law.

Bottom: Kaiser Jeep's Brazilian operation, known as Willys Overland do Brasil (WOB), produced a full line of passenger cars and Jeeps, including this handsome Rural station wagon, which was based on the U.S. Jeep station wagon, restyled for the local market.

Actor Rock Hudson is seen here struggling to pitch a tent, in a vain attempt to prove he's a real outdoorsman, in the comedy classic *Man's Favorite Sport.* His 1964 Jeep Wagoneer appears throughout the film.

Kaiser Jeep earned more than $11 million that year, while parent company Kaiser Industries reported much lower profits due to heavy losses at its Kaiser Engineers division.

By 1965 the market for four-wheel-drive vehicles was getting very competitive. International Harvester had entered the field for 1961 with its new Scout and also fielded a line of four-wheel-drive pickups and the Travelall station wagon. Toyota was grabbing customers with its quirky imported Land Cruiser, while British maker Rover offered its rugged Land Rover. Now for 1966 Ford Motor Company entered the fray with its sharp and capable Bronco SUV, which drew buyers who wanted more style and comfort than the CJ-5 could offer and yet didn't want a big four-door Wagoneer. In addition, the buying public was hankering for more power again; there was

a horsepower race going on in the passenger car market and one side result was that people also expected more power in their trucks and utility vehicles. Jeep responded by purchasing 155-horsepower V-6 engines from General Motors. These were originally designed for use in Buicks. When they were installed in CJs, the results were almost astounding. The formerly underpowered CJ-5 and CJ-6 could now do

As wife of a prominent Kaiser Jeep executive, Virginia Moss had her pick of the company's offerings, and one that she enjoyed a great deal was this Jeep Surrey. Note the Jeep still wears Willys wheel discs, dating the vehicle to a circa 1962 model.

four-wheel burnouts and had acceleration that was actually exhilarating. Kaiser Jeep was so pleased it ended up buying the V-6 engine tooling from GM.

Jeep Wagoneer received an attractive facelift partway through the model year when the keystone grille was chucked in favor of a handsome new full-width grille. Gladiators and panel trucks continued to use the old-style grille. A bit earlier, Wagoneer and Gladiator models also got a new engine, this one a lusty 250-horsepower 327-cid V-8 purchased from American Motors. It transformed the senior Jeeps into real performers. During the later part of the year, the company also phased in the American Motors 232-cid six as the standard engine for the senior lines; the Willys OHC engine was discontinued except for military vehicles.

Also debuting that year was an all-new Fleetvan, the FJ-6, which used a sharp-edged, angular body mated to a longer chassis. Few of these vehicles exist today and they are a rather interesting sidebar to Jeep history.

An interesting—and very frustrating—problem developed as a result of the new engines that were introduced. Dealers complained that buyers only wanted to buy Jeeps with the new powerplants, and leftover inventory with the older engines was sitting on their lots for months longer than normal. This affected the dealer's ability to order more stock units and caused a rather large drop in wholesale sales to dealers. It

The popular Jeep pickups could be had in a variety of wheelbases, models, and trims, including this rugged Stake Truck.

Top: A big part of Kaiser Jeep's income came from overseas sales of its products. This Toledo-built Jeep CJ-6 is being loaded onto a freighter for shipment to some faraway place. Jeep usually ranked third or fourth in U.S. vehicle export sales.

Many Jeeps were produced overseas in what are commonly called "screwdriver plants," places where the vehicle is assembled from parts rather than manufactured on the spot. It's not known if these boxes contain complete Jeep vehicles or parts kits for overseas assembly.

took months for the inventory to finally be sold off. The end result was that, even though Jeep sold more military vehicles that year, its profit dropped to just $4.9 million because retail sales were down. The military units had a lower profit margin than retail vehicles, thus the drop in earnings. And parent Kaiser Industries suffered a loss that year. The cause, once again, was problems in its engineering division.

But there were bright spots during the year. In overseas markets, IKA and Willys Overland do Brasil together sold more than 100,000 vehicles in South America, a remarkable record. The sales totals for the United States included an order for postal FJ-6 Fleetvan's along with a unique, little-known military Jeep designed especially for overseas markets, the budget-priced M-606. This was essentially a civilian CJ-3B with a few added military hardware items, such as a pintle hitch, olive drab paint, and blackout lights. It fit the bill for many foreign militaries looking for a low-priced tactical vehicle. In the U.S. retail market public acceptance of the repowered Jeeps was encouraging and seemed to bode well

for the future. Another big plus: At year end Jeep had a backlog of more than $420 million in government orders for military vehicles, an astounding sum for that time.

So although Jeep executives had some real concerns about Ford's entry into the four-wheel-drive utility market, overall the company entered the 1966 model year brimming with confidence. It had fresh products, a healthy order backlog, and with the Vietnam War heating up, plenty of prospects for even more government business.

This circa-1965 photo shows a group of soldiers climbing into a military Jeep M38-A1. Although the U.S. Army had since switched to the M-151 Mutt vehicle, there were still many of these durable M38-A1s still in service in many armies around the globe.

That confidence showed up in the newest model to debut from Jeep: the spectacular Super Wagoneer. This milestone vehicle was an all-out luxury version of the Wagoneer, with luxury interior trim and a comprehensive list of standard features, including a special 270-horsepower version of the Vigilante V-8, Hydra-Matic transmission, power brakes, power steering, air conditioning, tilt steering wheel, tinted glass, radio, and power tailgate window. The exterior was highlighted by antique gold and black trim panels on the sides and rear, spoke wheel covers, fender emblems, a vinyl top, and whitewall tires. Inside were plush bucket seats, full carpeting, a sports console, courtesy lights, and an acoustic headliner. The Super Wagoneer was revolutionary; it was the first luxury Sports Utility Vehicle ever. It set a new standard for SUVs that was unmatched and would not be approached for many years.

A big development came midyear when the company won a $91 million contract for more than 20,000 M-715 and M-725 trucks and ambulances. These were new models developed by Jeep engineers; essentially they were heavily altered and beefed-up versions of the Gladiator. An interesting point is that Jeep competed against two very large automakers for the job—on both an engineering basis and a low-bid basis—and was able to win the business, producing a superior truck at a price that undercut the big guys. Production was set to begin in January 1967.

For the 1966 fiscal year, Jeep reported sales of a whopping $322.9 million and a net profit of $7.1 million. This was the result of a 23 percent

The military M-170 Field Ambulance was a popular vehicle and the U.S. armed services bought thousands of them.

In April 1965, Kaiser Jeep Corporation announced the availability of the 250-horsepower "Vigilante" V-8 engine, optional in the J-series trucks and Wagoneers. Generating its peak torque of 340 foot-pounds at a low 2,600 rpm, this engine, produced by American Motors, was an ideal choice for off-road and on-road use.

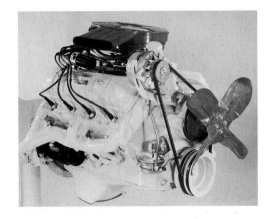

increase in military sales. Despite strong production in 1966 at year end, the company's backlog of government orders actually rose to $470 million. And the parent company was solidly profitable.

One could say that 1967 was the Year of the Jeepster because in January 1967 the company began heavily promoting and selling its newest products, the Jeepster and Jeepster Commando. Built on a Jeep CJ-6 chassis with a longer, much more stylish body, the Jeepster and Jeepster Commando were Kaiser Jeep's belated attempt to counter the threat from Ford Bronco and International Scout.

The Jeepster was offered in only a single model, a good-looking two-door convertible with roll-up windows and a fold-down convertible top, either manual or power-operated. Bucket seats and deluxe upholstery were standard equipment, as were a pair of bright metal moldings that ran from the base of the windshield down the sides and wrapping around the rear of the vehicle, with the inset part painted a contrasting color. It

was an upscale, sporty car for people who wanted a four-wheel-drive vehicle with more room and comfort than a CJ could offer.

Jeepster Commando, on the other hand, offered a full series of models that included a basic roadster with roll-up windows but no top, the same with a pull-off soft top, a pickup with either a soft top or steel hardtop, or a hardtop station wagon. The interior of the Jeepster Commando was rather plain, one could even call it stark, but buyers could dress it up with a

With the availability of the potent new V-8, Gladiator trucks became even better haulers than before, with plenty of power in reserve. This 1965 Gladiator is equipped with the V-8, as noted by the emblem on the front fender.

rear seat (standard on station wagons), Deluxe trim, floor console, tinted glass, and much more.

Unlike the original Jeepster, all Jeepsters and Jeepster Commandos came standard with four-wheel drive. The four-cylinder Hurricane engine was standard equipment, but most buyers chose the optional Dauntless V-6. Turbo Hydra-Matic transmission, air conditioning, and power brakes were all available, as was a power top for the Jeepster convertible.

The rest of the 1967 Jeep line was basically carryover with only minor mechanical improvements.

Success continued into 1967 with Kaiser Jeep reporting total sales of a record-setting $470.7 million and a total profit of more than $30 million. The actual operating profit was $14.5 million, which by itself was excellent, and the company reported a one-time gain of $16.4 million when it sold its interests in its two major South American affiliates, Industrias Kaiser Argentina, which was sold to Renault, and Willys-Overland do Brasil, which was sold to Ford Motor Company.

Why Kaiser Industries sold its highly profitable and growing South American companies is a bit puzzling. Partly it might be because the two were growing larger, maturing, and building more of the vehicles' parts in-house, which was reducing Kaiser's income from supplying parts to them. Or it might have been simply that good offers for the two companies came in around the same time and Mr. Kaiser decided to accept both and take some profits.

But there may have been an entirely different reason. A few years earlier, around 1961, George Romney of American Motors had investigated buying Kaiser Jeep, but eventually decided against it in order to focus AMC's resources on its core automobile business. Then, around 1964–65 his successor, Roy Abernethy, also looked into buying Jeep but concluded that the acquisition cost was simply too high for AMC to afford. A large part of the total cost was accounted for by Jeep's investment in IKA and WOB, so perhaps the Kaiser family decided they needed to sell those two companies separately in hopes they could then sell Jeep Corporation to AMC, or any other buyer they could find. It was a fact that Edgar Kaiser, Henry's son and chairman of Kaiser Industries, was tired of being in the car business and he greatly desired selling his Jeep

Left: The CJ-5 could take you and your boat just about anywhere. Its small size, narrow width, and unstoppable four-wheel drive meant it could weave through dense forests better than any other SUV.

Right: Here's a 1965 CJ-5 Tuxedo park, which Jeep called a "sports car," and it was indeed becoming thought of as a sports car for people who loved the outdoors and off-road adventuring.

One of the major advances in Jeep's business came with the expansion of its military sales beyond the simple M38-A1. In June 1966, the company announced it had won a major contract to supply the M-715 vehicles, a series of trucks based on a modified Jeep Gladiator. The nearly $91 million contract called for delivery of 20,680 vehicles. Seated at the wheel of this M-715 truck is Stephen Girard, president of Kaiser Jeep; standing next to him is executive vice president Cruse Moss.

operations. He saw troubles ahead. The retail end of the business was simply not growing as much as it needed to. His dealer network was neither large nor strong; sales of Jeep vehicles exclusive of government business totaled just 61,300 vehicles worldwide. Although that was up 11 percent over the prior fiscal year in light of the new products introduced, it was not a good number at all and probably not profitable.

How was Jeep faring in comparison to its competitors? That was all there to see if anyone cared to look. The truck market was in a rapid growth mode during the 1960s and overall sales of light trucks had nearly doubled from 1960 to 1966, while Jeep retail sales in the United States grew only 35 percent in the same period. Rival International Harvester's truck sales had grown more than 66 percent, while GMC's

had climbed 61 percent. Jeep was not only lagging the market, but it was lagging compared to its two rivals closest in size. The company was heading into trouble.

There was one rather ominous comment in the corporate annual report that escaped most people's attention. "Government business accounted for approximately two-thirds of the company's 1967 net sales and *the profitability of Kaiser Jeep Corporation is dependent on high-volume military production.*" (Italics added.) What company management was saying quite plainly was that the retail part of Jeep's business wasn't profitable. The company had become wholly dependent on military and other government sales. That was all right for the present, with a nasty war raging in Southeast Asia, but what would happen if the

military began to wind down its purchasing? Would Jeep begin to bleed to death? By January 1968 Jeep had an order backlog of $350 million, down substantially from the prior year but a healthy amount nonetheless. The company had enough military work to last until September 1969. One could be forgiven for asking: What then?

During 1967, sadness came to the Kaiser family when its patriarch Henry J. Kaiser died on August 24. His was the passing of a giant of industry, one of the remarkable legends of American business and one of the greatest can-do individuals of all time.

For 1968 Jeep added a new model to the Jeepster Commando line, a low-priced convertible that used a different soft top than the high-line Jeepster and could be had as either a manual or power top. Other than that, the Jeepsters were essentially carryover. The Wagoneer line saw some important changes. During the year, the slow-selling two-wheel-drive models were dropped

from the lineup, as were the even slower-selling two-door models. The AMC 327-cid V-8 was phased out and in its place came a 350-cid Buick V-8, dubbed the "Dauntless V-8." Also during that year, the elegant Super Wagoneer was phased out due to slow sales; apparently it was simply too far ahead of its time. A new Custom Wagoneer model debuted—nicely trimmed though much less extravagant than the Super and quite a bit less costly.

In the truck line the Gladiators also got the new Buick-sourced Dauntless V-8; at 230 horsepower, this engine was less powerful than the AMC 327 V-8, but you weren't supposed to notice that. During the year, the company phased out the two-wheel-drive Gladiator models, as well as the panel truck, in order to concentrate resources on its core market of four-wheel-drive vehicles. In addition, the long-wheelbase models no longer offered the Thriftside bed. Other than that, there wasn't much new in trucks for 1968.

Another major advance was this Jeep Super Wagoneer, the first-ever luxury SUV. The lengthy list of standard features and elegant trim and interior fittings made this the best sports utility wagon you could buy, and a highly desirable collectible today.

Although U.S. retail sales fell slightly, Kaiser Jeep reported its best year ever for 1968. Sales totaled $476.9 million and an operating profit of more than $15 million was earned. The company noted once again that the excellent financial numbers were the result of high-volume production of military vehicles and that profitability for 1969 would again be dependent on government orders. Nongovernment unit sales fell 3 percent, partly because of a drop in overseas business and partly because of faltering sales of the Jeepster line, a bad sign for so new a product. Fewer than 13,000 1968 Jeepster Commando's had been built.

The final year of the decade, 1969, was destined to be a memorable one for Kaiser Jeep Corporation. It wasn't all that great sales-wise. Unit sales in the United States for the calendar year came to just 36,000 Jeeps, but the company did launch a new truck model, a Gladiator on a 132-inch wheelbase designed specifically for carrying a camper. Recreational use of four-wheel-drive vehicles was one of many factors driving the market higher and higher and Jeep simply wasn't sharing in that growth, so the company turned its focus in 1969 to pitching Jeeps for camping use. A

new camper for the CJ was also unveiled, and although it was rather small it somehow managed to contain all the necessities of camp living while providing a warm, dry place to sleep in. Naturally enough, Wagoneers were touted as being ideal for towing trailers.

Toward the end of the year, Edgar Kaiser met quietly with Roy D. Chapin Jr., CEO of American Motors, to discuss the idea of AMC purchasing Kaiser Jeep Corporation. The two men were old acquaintances and the discussions were friendly. After all, Kaiser knew that Chapin had for nearly a decade wanted AMC to buy Jeep, and Chapin knew that Kaiser wanted to

In 1951, Willys began production of its newest military model, the MD, which the armed forces designated the M38-A1. It offered a potent F-head engine, more room, better ride, more carrying capacity, and several other improvements. Here we see the MD undergoing proving ground testing in Aberdeen, Maryland, the same place where the original Jeep was first tested.

sell, so all that really needed to be worked out was the price. It would be substantially lower than it had been in earlier talks because in the meantime the company had sold off its two big South America affiliates, and also was suffering stagnant retail sales in the U.S. market. In addition, military vehicle contracts were getting harder to obtain, and without those Jeep would begin to lose money, lots of it. By this point, the company had government orders going into 1970, but everyone knew that once the Vietnam War ended, military spending would be slashed, hurting Jeep.

There was another reason for selling Jeep that loomed larger than all that. The Kaisers had always considered themselves engineers, miners of raw materials, people who extracted things from the earth. The Kaiser-Frazer car business launched in 1946 had quickly turned into a headache, and then became a disaster for which the only salvation was to buy another car

Left: This circa 1967 Jeep CJ-5 apparently had several roles: a jaunty roadster for enjoying early spring drives in the country, and a snow plow in the winter—notice the plow setup behind the front bumper.

Bottom: Jeepster offered the only true convertible in the Jeep lineup in 1967; a convertible wasn't offered in the Commando series, only a roadster with optional pull-off soft top. The Jeepster's standard top was manually operated, but a power top could be ordered.

company to prop them up. Thus they had ended up owning Jeep, and even though it was generally their largest and most profitable division, the family was tired of owning it and wanted out. The auto industry simply wasn't their kind of business. Edgar Kaiser would hold out for as much money as he could get, but in the end he would sell Jeep no matter what. There were no other companies interested in Jeep at the time, because it had become such a marginal player in the retail market, especially in the United States.

In the end, Chapin and Kaiser hammered out a deal that was fair to both sides. In exchange for a dwindling vehicle company that just happened to be one of the best-known brands in the world, Chapin paid $10 million in cash, $9.49 million in interest-bearing five-year notes, and 5,500,000 shares of AMC stock. The total package was valued at roughly $70 million. The Kaisers recorded the transaction as an $8.5

Top: The 1967 Wagoneer. This year Kaiser Jeep reported sales of $470.7 million, a new record, and a profit of more than $30 million. The company sold its interests in its two major South American affiliates, Industrias Kaiser Argentina and Willys Overland do Brasil.

Middle: Here we see a total of four 1968 Jeep models at an unnamed auto show. The building doesn't look familiar and the display is small. Does anyone out there recognize it?

Bottom: Here we see the 1968 Jeep Super Wagoneer, still the most luxurious four-wheel drive on the market. The factory sales catalogs don't show this model available after 1968, but apparently a small number were, though they might have been leftover 1968s that were retitled as 1969s.

million dollar loss on the book value of Jeep's physical assets and used the cash they received to pay down Kaiser Industries' debt. They knew they would have to hold onto the AMC stock for a while.

Because of the large holdings of AMC stock it now had—equal to roughly 22 percent ownership of the company—Kaiser Industries was given two seats on AMC's board of directors. In press statements, both Chapin and Kaiser repeatedly emphasized that Kaiser Industries was not interested in acquiring American Motors, and on a more personal side, Roy Chapin had Edgar Kaiser's word of honor that he wouldn't attempt a takeover. The whole reason for using stock to purchase Jeep was for AMC to conserve its hard cash; the company was still struggling to gain traction after nearly going bankrupt a few years earlier.

Despite having purchased Jeep at a good price, Roy D. Chapin was not a hero to everyone. His own company had come perilously close to insolvency in 1967 and was not yet out of the woods. It was only marginally profitable and

Left: The 1969 four-wheel-drive Jeep CJ-5. Although the company still offered the DJ-5 two-wheel-drive model, it did not advertise or even actively market it. It wasn't a good sales year for Jeep. Unit sales in the United States came to just 36,000 vehicles.

Bottom: In 1969, Jeep put a great deal of emphasis on Jeeps for recreational use, such as camping and hunting. The Gladiator line added a heavy-duty model on a 132-inch wheelbase designed specifically for carrying a camper.

Above: There was even a camper for the CJ series, though not many were sold. As small as it was, the little camper had all the comforts of home.

Bottom: The 1969 Wagoneer Custom has an elegant woodgrain side spear, full-wheel discs, and chrome roof rack. Wagoneer was an ideal vehicle that rode smoothly on pavement yet could conquer the toughest off-road terrain.

could easily slip into unprofitability with just a minor downturn in sales. It was in no shape to take on a potential money-loser. And even Chapin's lieutenants were not all behind him on the purchase. AMC vice president Gerald C. Meyers, the point man who inspected Jeep prior to the sale, said in his report that he recommended against purchasing Jeep.

"I felt we had enough problems on our plate already and didn't need to go out and acquire more," he later recalled. Many in the press saw the Jeep purchase as a huge mistake; the influential business magazine *Dun's Review* even called it "Chapin's Folly."

The signing and final consummation of the transaction was a bit complicated. The deal was first announced on October 20, 1969. Then, the two firms signed an agreement

December 2, 1969, with the understanding that it had to be approved by Kaiser and American Motors stockholders before it could go into effect. Once approval was gotten from both boards, it was backdated to September 30, 1969, so that Kaiser Jeep's financial numbers for the last three months of the year could be included in AMC's 1970 fiscal year, which began October 1, 1969.

So at long last Roy D. Chapin finally achieved what he had been trying to accomplish for so many years: the merging of the operations of American Motors and Jeep. Despite all the naysayers, Chapin was supremely confident that the two companies were a perfect fit. As head of AMC's international efforts in the early 1960s, he had seen how partnerships with Jeep had worked wonderful economies of scale in foreign markets, including Mexico, Argentina, and Venezuela, along with other smaller markets. And he had seen how offering

Left: Shown here is a previously unseen prototype proposal for a restyled Wagoneer. The attempt here is to make it appear more elegant. It is an interesting design but was ultimately rejected.

Right: Another Jeep project was this XJ-002 prototype, designed and built by an outside firm. Based on a Jeepster Commando six-cylinder chassis, the idea was that an owner could use the vehicle to drive to work during the week and then race it off-road on weekends. The concept was rejected.

Bottom: Realizing that the Jeepster was no match for the larger and better trimmed Bronco and Blazer, Jeep began exploring possibilities for a new vehicle to replace it. The cut-down Wagoneer body on the right was one idea that almost made it. In the end, American Motors would use roughly the same concept when it created the first Cherokee.

two distinctly different types of vehicles created synergies with both companies. Chapin knew that Jeep would grow to become a good profit maker for American Motors. All he had to do now was keep AMC afloat while trying to integrate two very different companies together, all within the background of the remorseless automobile business. It would be no easy task, but thankfully American Motors had a good team assembled to get the job done. Together they would engineer a miracle of business that would become an industry legend.

CHAPTER 4

The final year in which postal and military Jeeps were produced by Jeep Corporation was 1970. The following year they came under the purview of a spin-off subsidiary known as AM General Corporation. Shown is a DJ-5A Dispatcher postal truck.

1970–1987

AMERICAN MOTORS TAKES THE WHEEL

WAS THE PURCHASE OF JEEP A GOOD DEAL for American Motors, or had the company bought itself a plate full of trouble? That was the question innumerable financial and automotive analysts were pondering in 1970. On the surface, the numbers didn't look good. Retail sales of Jeep vehicles in the United States were in a decline, coming to less than 34,000 units during calendar year 1970, and that side of the business lost money. Government and overseas vehicle sales were better, but how much they offset the retail group's losses is difficult to say.

However, the deal was done, so now it was up to Roy Chapin and his executives to make it work. Chapin assigned Gerry Meyers to the task of integrating Jeep operations into AMC's. Vice president Marvin Stuckey was put in charge of re-engineering the Jeep lineup to integrate as many AMC components as possible while also upgrading the vehicles NVH (noise, vibration, and harshness) characteristics. The AMC engineers were surprised at how antiquated the Jeep's engineering actually was. The Hurricane four-cylinder used in the Universal and Commando dated back to the 1930s and had last been updated in 1950, so by 1970 it was positively ancient and sadly underpowered. The V-6, while modern and powerful, suffered from a rough idle due to its basic design. Chassis-wise, the consensus was that each vehicle would need a complete redesign, which would have to be done over a period of a few years since the cost was going to be considerable. In addition, Gerry Meyers wanted to retool the Universal's body to make it easier to assemble and improve its quality. AMC engineers had their work cut out for them.

American Motors tried to come up with a more stylish hardtop for the CJ-5 to replace the plain steel top that was then offered. This mockup, which also displays hood stripes and a special interior, was one idea created by AMC stylists.

THE COMPANY ALSO NEEDED to weed out the smaller, weaker Jeep dealers—of which there were plenty—and replace them with more-solid, better-financed AMC dealers, because the Jeep distribution system was simply not up to industry standards. Jeep's declining retail performance was all there to see in black and white in the industry sales rankings. In 1960, before the truck market began to take off, Jeep managed to retail 31,385 vehicles in the United States, while its peer Dodge sold 31,344 units, and GMC and International Harvester sold 45,761 and 48,729, respectively. By 1969, Jeep U.S. sales had risen to just 36,017 units, while GMC sold 101,189, IH sold 63,480, and Dodge

sold a whopping 127,296. In a market that was growing strongly, Jeep was simply treading water. A more modern distribution network was one of the remedies that AMC could supply.

Obviously, there was nothing substantive that AMC could do to improve the 1970 Jeep vehicles, since they were already on sale. The Wagoneer did receive a scheduled grille change midyear, along with a new sliding steel sunroof option. The Gladiator trucks also received a new grille, the one that was just replaced from the Wagoneer. which went a long way toward modernizing the truck's appearance. Side marker lights, first installed in 1969, were better integrated on all vehicles for 1970. Trucks

Here's a neat optical illusion by Jeep stylists. Shown is a mockup for a vehicle called the Commando II, a forerunner of the 1974 Cherokee. Only half of the grille was produced; the other half is actually a mirror image. Note the backward numbers on the license plate. If you look closely, you can see the edges of the mirror. This trick was done to speed up development of new ideas, since it required less work than creating a full grille design.

The 1971 Jeep Gladiator truck, with the new grille that debuted during 1970. The two-tone paint and Westcoast mirrors give this J3000 real style to go with its rugged nature. Note the attractive bed cover too.

In 1971, AMC spun off Jeep's commercial, postal, and military product line into its new AM General subsidiary, with Jeep veteran Cruse Moss in command. The company still exists today.

offered a side-mounted spare tire, though it ended up causing problems when trying to maneuver in tight spaces. The Jeepster line now offered power steering, something it really needed because the number of turns lock-to-lock with the manual steering were excessive. Surprisingly, both the DJ-5 and DJ-6 two-wheel-drive models remained in production and were available through any Jeep dealer, though they were generally not shown in sales catalogs.

Perhaps the most significant model in the 1970 Jeep lineup was the new CJ-5 Renegade I, a very limited production sporty version of the Universal. Featuring the V-6 engine and bucket seats, the Renegade stood out partly because it was offered in only two bright colors: Wild Plum and Mint Green (some sources list red as a third choice), but mostly because it was so unusual to see a Jeep configured as a sports vehicle. Equipment included 8-inch-wide white steel wheels, big G70x15 tires, a roll bar, a swing-away spare tire carrier, a Trac-Lok limited-slip rear axle, and an oil pressure gauge. Estimates of how many Renegade Is were built range from 250 to 500 units. The

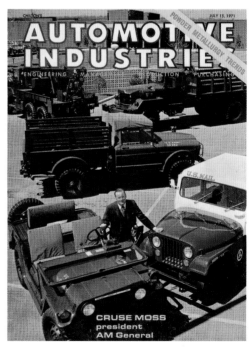

Renegade I was influenced by the positive reception given in 1969 to another very limited-production CJ dubbed the "462," which featured a standard roll bar, V-6 engine, and bucket seats.

There were two special vehicle design programs left over from the Kaiser era. The Jeep XJ-001 was a concept created by Jeep desi-

One the most exciting Jeeps of the 1970s was the limited-production Hurst Jeepster, of which it's believed only 100 were built. Shown is an all-original vehicle purchased new in California and still in the same family.

gn chief Jim Anger for a four-wheel-drive Jeep sports car and featured a low-slung two-seat body with scooped-out door openings and a V-8 engine mounted on a Jeep CJ chassis. The second vehicle, dubbed the XJ-002, was created by an outside firm. Like the XJ-001, it was a two-seat sports car, this time built on a six-cylinder Jeepster Commando chassis.

Kaiser Jeep had segregated its nonretail business in a unit called the Defense and Government Products Division, and AMC renamed it the General Products Division, with the very capable Cruse Moss in charge. The division introduced a new postal Jeep, the Dispatcher 100, with a lighter unitized body, powered by a Chevy four-cylinder engine.

Trying to integrate Jeep and AMC together proved to be a time-consuming and costly challenge, and for 1970 American Motors reported a loss of $56.2 million, a near-ruinous deficit for a company in AMC's financial condition. But Roy Chapin was unfazed, assuring stockholders that "Jeep can be and will be a major profit contributor to American Motors." Opponents of the merger smugly

repeated their I-told-you-sos to anyone who would listen.

The 1971 line of Jeep vehicle debuted in the fall of 1970. There wasn't a whole lot of change apparent, but as the year progressed changes and improvements began to show up. The AMC 258-cid six-cylinder engine replaced the smaller 232-cid as the standard mill in Wagoneer and Gladiator models, while the AMC 304-cid and 360-cid V-8s replaced the Buick V-8. During the year, brilliant Roy Lunn of Ford GT40 fame joined Jeep Engineering, charged with the task

American Motors product planners realized they needed a larger vehicle than the Commando, so they began to develop one from the old Wagoneer two-door body shell. This running mockup bears the name "Commando."

of completely revamping the Jeep product line. He would go on to earn great fame at Jeep.

Meanwhile, Jeep's new Product Planning group had noticed that the special models previously developed by Kaiser, primarily the sporty 462 and Renegade I, moved off the dealer lots more quickly than standard units did. The Renegade I had sold out almost immediately on introduction. So for 1971, several special limited-production models were introduced, including the Renegade II, which was similar to the first iteration but now came with gorgeous alloy wheels and four body colors. Of these, 200 Renegade IIs were produced in Baja Yellow, 200 in Mint Green, 50 in Riverside Orange, and 150 in Big Bad Orange. All of these were quickly sold and many potential buyers were left empty handed. In the Jeepster line, there were two special models, the SC-1, which featured the V-6 engine, radio, roof rack, and sporty wheel covers. It was offered in just one color, Butterscotch Gold with a white roof. The other special Jeepster was the Hurst Jeepster Special, an all-white Jeepster wagon with minor modifications by Hurst Performance. These included rally stripes and a hood-mounted tachometer. The only engine offered was the V-6,

which could be hooked up to either a manual or automatic transmission, both equipped with a special Hurst shifter. It's believed that only 100 of the Hurst Jeepster's were built and the model today is one of the hottest collectible Jeep vehicles.

The product planners were investigating other ideas as well. One planner, Jim Alexander, came up with an idea for a compact Jeep pickup truck he called the Cowboy. It was based on a cut-down two-door AMC Hornet passenger car body, with a stub rear frame carrying a 6-foot pickup bed. Three were built; a nonrunning fiberglass mock-up, a six-cylinder test car, and a test car built on a Hornet SC/360 V-8. Of these, only the V-8 car survives. The program was seriously considered for production when an unforeseen snag developed; sales of AMC's Gremlin and Hornet were so hot from 1973 to 1975 the company couldn't build enough to meet demand. That left no room on the assembly lines for the Cowboy, which languished and finally was dropped. Product planners also began to investigate producing a sport utility wagon that was larger than the slow-selling Commando. Big vehicles such as the Chevy Blazer and Ford Bronco were grabbing the bulk of the two-door SUV market and it was time for Jeep to field a proper competitor.

The slide in Jeep retail sales was finally halted during 1971, though the result—just 35,925 U.S. retail sales during the calendar year—was nothing to brag about. However, with the Jeep dealer network getting stronger every day from the influx of new dealers and the continual weeding out of weak ones, and with the help of new trim and equipment options coming out from the factory, it was hoped that the following year would see a significant increase in sales.

Roy D. Chapin Jr. created a whole new company in 1971 when he spun off the General Products Division into a separate corporation, with Cruse Moss at the helm. Moss named his new company AM General; Chapin told him his mission was to grow the business, and also to take it into new market segments. Extremely competent, Moss, a longtime veteran from Kaiser Jeep, was only too happy to comply. He set about investigating the bus market.

For 1972 there were more mechanical changes and improvements in the Jeep lineup than there had been in several years. The DJ-5, CJ-5, and CJ-6 series bodies were redesigned for easier assembly and improved quality. The frame and front-end sheet metal were lengthened to accommodate installation of the AMC 232-cid six-cylinder engine as standard

equipment, with the 258-cid six and the mighty 304 V-8 as new options. The new standard six was smooth, quiet, and a lot more powerful than the hoary old Hurricane four, and it had a solid reputation for durability. The optional 258-cid six added a bit more punch to the smaller Jeeps. But the 304 V-8 transformed the CJ into a real powerhouse and it quickly became the option of choice for hardcore off-roaders. In addition, CJ brakes were improved and a higher-capacity heater was installed. A new front axle allowed for a shorter turning radius. Power steering and power brakes were other new options. We should note that when the decision was made to retool the CJ body, there was some discussion about changing its styling to make the CJ's look fresh and more modern. However, in the end Gerry Meyers decided to retain the "classic" Jeep look.

In the senior line, the Gladiator name was dropped. The pickups were now known simply as Jeep Trucks and they came in six models: J-2500 and J-3500 on a 120-inch wheelbase and J4500, J-4600, J-4700, and J-4800 on a 132-inch wheelbase. Jeep Wagoneer's offered standard carpeting and a standard rear seat; both of these were optional on competitor's vehicles.

Jeep usually pitched the Wagoneer as a family station wagon, emphasizing its extra margin of safety via its four-wheel drive and its overall usefulness.

In an effort to boost lagging sales of the Jeepster Commando, Jeep stylists created this special SC-1 model, which was available on a limited basis during 1971. The package included stripes, roof rack, custom wheel covers, and custom interior trim. The only color available was Butterscotch, a brilliant shade of orange.

The most popular model in the Jeepster Commando line was the station wagon, such as the 1971 model shown here. The hardtop is removable and the vehicle can seat four passengers. By this point, the convertible models had been dropped.

Continuing its theme of Jeep CJ-5 as a sports machine, Jeep offered hood side stripes, whitewall tires, and full-wheel discs as options to dress up the vehicle. The chrome bumper shown here was also an option, as was the roll bar.

The CJ-5 Renegade returned, still as a limited-production model available only part of the model year. In 1972, it nearly wore the Renegade III designation, in keeping with past practice, but a management decision came down to shorten the name to just Renegade. There were three color choices that year: Renegade Plum, Renegade Orange, and Renegade Yellow.

The Jeepster was renamed the Jeep Commando, and like the CJs, the series got a longer chassis and front sheet metal and used the same engine lineup as the smaller brethren. In addition, the Commando now boasted a completely restyled front end, which made it look larger and more modern than before. The last major styling effort by Kaiser Jeep designer Jim Anger, who came to AMC with the merger, the new look was controversial from the start. It was attractive, but did it look like a Jeep? There was another limited-edition Jeep Commando model for 1972, the seldom-seen SC-2, which featured a woodgrain side stripe. How many were produced is unknown, but they are extremely rare today.

The turnaround in Jeep sales volume that began in 1971 speeded up in 1972, with retail sales coming in at 50,926 for the calendar year (46,000 during the AMC fiscal year, which ended on September 30). The company lumped overseas car and Jeep sales together, and no reliable breakout has been found thus far, but it appears there was an increase in overseas Jeep deliveries as well. The truck market was continuing its rapid growth and analysts predicted that 1973 would be another record year.

By the end of 1972, Jeep sales were growing by leaps and bounds and it continued into the 1973 model year. The 1973 lineup was particularly strong. The biggest news was the availability of a completely new type of four-wheel drive called Quadra-Trac. This was a full-time system in which each wheel could operate at its own speed without putting undue strain on the driveline, thus allowing smooth operation even on hard, dry surfaces. That meant that the four-wheel drive could now operate all the time (full time), eliminating the need to use the transfer case lever except when engaging low range for severe off-road usage while eliminating lock-out hubs entirely.

It opened up the four-wheel-drive market to many thousands of people intimidated by the shift levers and lock-out hubs that conventional four-wheel-drive vehicles had. This was a major advance in four-wheel-drive technology, one that AMC vice president Marvin Stuckey called "...as significant to the four-wheel-drive vehicle as the first automatic transmission was to the automobile." And that was no overstatement. The new four-wheel-drive system was one of the crowning accomplishments in the industry's history, because it opened up the market so broadly. Initially, Quadra-Trac was available only on Wagoneer's equipped with the 360-cid V-8 and automatic transmission, but in time it was also offered on trucks. It was such a revolutionary advance it was sure to find its way onto other Jeep vehicles as well.

In addition to Quadra-Trac, the senior Jeeps also got a new instrument panel, energy-absorbing steering column, new oil and ammeter gauges, a new steering wheel, and broad changes in upholstery and trim. Trucks also got a new double wall Townside pickup box with a single-handle latch and a tailgate opening that was nearly 3 inches wider.

The CJ line saw numerous mechanical improvements, including "soft feel" control knobs with international symbols, a relocated parking brake release, lighted heater controls, and new standard electric windshield wipers with integrated washer. The Commando also got these changes, plus new optional sliding quarter windows in the station wagon.

During the year, some crafty American rally drivers decided to enter a pair of Jeep Wagoneers in off-road rallying against more traditional European competitors, such as Lancia, Saab, and Audi. To everyone's surprise, the Wagoneers proved to be nearly unbeatable, quickly winning the Press-On-Regardless Rally and the 13-hour SCCA Sno-Drift Rally. Fans of European sports sedans were incensed, to say the least, that these big American

In late 1971, AMC designer Jim Alexander created a new Jeep truck concept by having an AMC Hornet SC-360 two-door sedan cut in half. A stub-frame was attached to the back half, upon which a 6-foot pickup bed was mounted. Called the Cowboy, only three were built: this nonrunning fiberglass mockup plus a yellow six-cylinder model and the SC360 V-8. Only the V-8 truck survives.

One problem with the CJ-5 was that it didn't have enough room to fit an automatic transmission. Shown here is a circa 1972 attempt to create a longer CJ that could take an automatic and also provide more interior space. This one may have been built on a CJ-6 chassis.

machines could best their highly developed rally cars.

Jeep's U.S. retail sales for calendar year 1973 set a record with 68,227 sold. That was excellent news, but for some people, however, it was time to eat a little crow. In an interview with the Detroit Auto Writers Group (DAWG), vice president Gerry Meyers admitted that "Jeep sales are so far beyond our planning volumes I'm embarrassed. I called Jeep 'Chapin's Folly' when we bought it." In the end, Meyers had to admit "Chapin was right." With money pouring in from both its Jeep and passenger car operations, American Motors reported a hefty profit for 1973 of just under $86 million, also a new record.

About the only thing that was bothering Meyers, besides trying to build more Jeeps, was that Chevy Blazer was taking about 50 percent of the sports utility wagon market, while Jeep Commando had a minor share. Meyers was determined to field a more

competitive sports wagon and he had his product planners working on the problem. He vowed to introduce a new Jeep for 1974 that would be more competitive.

The Jeep line for 1974 had a new tone of confidence. The company now held 18 percent of the total four-wheel-drive market, and its growth potential was strong. The Jeep CJ-5 offered its Renegade package as a regular production option, thus making one of the most profitable and desirable CJ options available all year-round. There were two Renegade colors

There were discussions among Jeep product planners and designers about changing and updating the look of the CJ-5, and shown here is one of the ideas for doing so. Luckily, somebody smart realized that the CJ series had the sort of iconic look that every designer strives for, so when the body was retooled for 1972 there was essentially no change to its appearance.

for 1974, Renegade Plum and Renegade Yellow, but the vehicle could also be ordered in any of the regular production colors. CJ sales (as well as passenger car sales) were so strong that the company was running short of six-cylinder engines to meet demand. Executives began considering a plan to reintroduce the old V-6 engine. They would have been installed in CJ's as an option, and possibly even in some passenger car models as well. In the end, the company decided to concentrate on increasing production of their own six.

As it continued an ongoing effort to morph into a true luxury SUV, the 1974 Wagoneer

got a stylish new grille, along with a standard 360-V-8 engine, automatic transmission, power steering, and power front disc brakes, plus Quadra-Trac full-time four-wheel drive. Two models were offered, standard and Custom, though the Custom was by far the better seller.

Jeep trucks were now identified as J-10 (½-ton) and J-20 (¾- ton) models. Within each series, there were various chassis, tire, and suspension options so that a variety of GVW ratings could be had. The J-20 offered GVWs up to a whopping 8,000 pounds. The AMC 401-cid V-8 was now available on trucks and Wagoneers.

Roy Lunn's engineering team was hard at work redesigning Jeep's underpinnings. All senior Jeeps received a new, stronger frame in 1974, with heavier side rails, open-end front axles for shorter turning radius, and fully insulated body mounts for a smoother, quieter ride.

But the big news for 1974 by far was the new Jeep sport utility wagon that would take on the Chevy Blazer and Ford Bronco. The Commando was dropped from the lineup, replaced there by the all-new Jeep Cherokee, a two-door SUV designed to outdo the competition. Cherokee was essentially the

Top: There nearly was a Renegade III model for 1973, and this is what it might have looked like. In the end, marketing and product planning could see that the Renegade was too popular to keep as a limited-production job, so for 1973 the Renegade became a regular offering in the CJ line, with a stripe pattern much different from this.

Bottom: AMC Jeep designer Chuck Mashigan came up with an idea for what he dubbed the "Space Capsule," a Jeep truck with a color-matched camper shell, seen here towing a CJ-5 concept vehicle called the Papoose.

The 1972 Renegade came with an American Motors 304-cid V-8 engine, which gave it amazing pulling power off-road and great acceleration on road. The V-8 could be ordered on other CJs as well. This Renegade is particularly attractive in its Renegade Plum paint.

Seen inside the Jeep Styling Studio at AMC headquarters in Detroit, this is the ultra-rare 1972 Jeep Commando SC-2, a limited-production model that arrived one year after the SC-1. The side moldings are unique to this model and outline a woodgrain side spear. Not many were sold, and it's not known if any have survived. This photo has never before been shown to the public.

old two-door Wagoneer model with a revised roof and grille, and with the sort of trim packages and marketing skill necessary to make it a winner in the marketplace. Unlike that on the Blazer and Bronco, Cherokee's roof was fixed, not removable, which made for a quieter cabin and a much safer vehicle. Cherokee was roomy inside, but its exterior dimensions were less imposing than the Blazer's and it was much easier to maneuver in traffic. Front bucket seats and a fold-down rear seat were standard equipment. The rear seat was an option on the Blazer, but other than that the base Cherokee was nearly as starkly equipped as its competitors, with rubber floor mats and

dog-dish hubcaps. What made Cherokee so desirable were its optional trims, especially the Cherokee S model, which included chrome bumpers, beautiful alloy wheels, special side appliqués, cut-pile carpeting, fancier upholstery, and special instrument panel trim. A tilt steering wheel, V-8 engines, and an automatic transmission were all available, as was Quadra-Trac, which made the Cherokee ideal as a family's main vehicle. AMC was able to price it competitively while still earning a handsome profit because the actual tooling bill had been next to nothing. Cherokee included so much of the old Wagoneer that only the roof and some small pieces had to be redesigned. In time Cherokee would become one of AMC's most profitable vehicles ever.

Although the U.S. truck market and the overall vehicle market were down considerably in 1974, during the calendar year Jeep dealers retailed 96,835 units in America, a solid gain and another new record. AMC's total sales volume topped the $2 billion mark, but inflation reared its ugly head during the year and costs for components and raw materials began to climb. The net effect was to depress American

Motors' profits to $27.5 million for the year, a letdown because record profits had been within reach. A big part of the problem was a strike in AMC's passenger car plants, which halted car production at a critical time. In overseas markets a new Jeep joint-venture affiliate was established to produce Jeeps in South Korea.

With the world slipping deeper into recession, the 1975 model year was bound to be more difficult than 1974. Inflation continued to rise, the economy sank, and many workers found themselves on the unemployment line. As component and raw material prices continued to soar, vehicle prices were rising as well, which greatly hindered sales. The truck market, which had begun to shrink during 1974, retreated even further that year, as did the overall market.

Despite the difficulties in the market, Jeep continued to enhance its product line for 1975, with all models getting electronic ignition and engine modifications to improve fuel economy. There were sharp new graphics for the CJ-5 Renegade, and all CJs were given a stronger frame, improved exhaust system, better engine insulation, and, finally, a standard passenger side bucket seat. It had always been optional. Windshield frames were now painted body color rather than black, and new optional Levi's-look seat upholstery debuted, in blue or tan. The Levi's

trim was standard on the Renegade and optional on other CJs. The optional AM radio was now factory-installed, rather than dealer-installed.

Cherokee sales were on fire, with most units being sold with a heavy load of optional equipment. The more loaded they were, the more money the company made so Jeep added many new items to the option list, including AM-FM radio with four speakers, rear window defogger, and cruise control. Buyers were demanding still more luxury items for their Cherokees.

Jeep trucks debuted a new trim package called the Pioneer, available on both J-10s and J-20s. The Pioneer package offered woodgrain trim on the instrument panel, interior door panels, and exterior bodysides, plus pleated fabric seats, deep pile carpeting, chrome front bumper, and more.

Jeep Wagoneer saw continued improvement for 1975, with a sharp new woodgrain side trim option, plus new standard features that included a light group, carpeting, custom seat trim and door panels, custom wheel covers, and a woodgrain instrument panel overlay. All senior Jeeps were given new springs and shocks for a better ride and improved handling,

The Jeepster Commando became the Jeep Commando in 1972 and the front-end sheet metal was completely redesigned. Styled by Jim Angers, this was an attempt to make the Commando look larger, since its toughest competitors were significantly bigger vehicles. The styling remains controversial to this day.

Although as trucks go the Jeep Commando wasn't all that practical, it was one of the best-looking pickups of that era and is quite desirable today. This is a 1972 model, showing the new frontal styling.

Jeep trucks continued with the same styling for 1973 but offered new optional equipment. The two-tone paint and side stripe really give this truck a look of excitement. The trucks got a new instrument panel this year and some interior redesign as well.

A beautiful sky, a beautiful woman, and a beautiful Jeep: Life doesn't get much better. Shown is a 1973 CJ-5 in fairly basic trim, though it does have optional side steps, more aggressive tires, and locking hubs. Judging by the mud spattered underneath it, this Jeep has seen some rough usage. But that's what Jeeps are made for.

an improved power steering system, and an improved defroster.

Who would ever have guessed that so minor an announcement would have so great an impact on the fortunes of one company? At the Detroit Auto Show in January 1975, Jeep unveiled a new Cherokee model called the Chief. It was scheduled to go into limited production in February and featured numerous sport and dress-up items. Most prominent were the wheel flares, wider axles, and big 8-inch wide spoke wheels, all of which gave it an aggressive look. Also neat were the 10-15 Goodyear Tracker A/T tires, special two-tone paint and stripe treatment, sports steering wheel, and an abundance of special trim. The Chief was priced at $349 extra on a Cherokee S, or $649 extra on the base Cherokee. From the moment it arrived, it was quickly sold out, with dealers hollering for more. Although no one realized it at the time, the Cherokee Chief was destined to become one of the most beloved Jeeps of all time.

But the economy continued to worsen in 1975 and it affected Jeep sales. Despite the many new features, 1975 ended up being a

down year for Jeep, as retail sales in the United States fell to 85,111. Although AMC's total sales volume climbed to $2.28 billion, the company reported a net loss of $27.5 million. Jeep operations were profitable for the year, but they couldn't hope to offset the horrendous losses in the passenger car division.

For 1976 Jeep Corporation unveiled yet another new model with broad appeal, the remarkable CJ-7. Built on a 10-inch longer chassis, the newest CJ's extra length provided a smoother ride, better handling, and provided enough room so that an automatic transmission could be fitted, along with Quadra-Trac four-wheel drive. Like the CJ-5, the CJ-7 came as an open roadster, with a soft top optional. But unlike the CJ-5 the new Jeep's optional hardtop was a better-looking and lighter polycarbonate top with steel doors, large windows. The CJ-7 was roomier, quieter, and even had storage space behind its rear seat, making it yet another vehicle that could serve as a family's primary car. Product planner Jim Alexander described it as a spiritual replacement for the old Commando. In any event, the public went wild over it and Jeep sales resumed their upward climb.

Jeep CJ models got new energy-absorbing steering columns with anti-theft ignition, new

steering wheels, and taillights, plus new instrument panels that provided space for an in-dash radio. A stronger three-speed manual gearbox also debuted. In a further demonstration of how utility vehicles were changing, the year's new options included a décor group, clock, and sports steering wheel. The popular Renegade package, which no longer included the V-8 engine, was available on both CJ-5 and CJ-7. With the introduction of the CJ-7, the CJ-6, which had never enjoyed much popularity in the United States, was discontinued in America and Canada. It remained in production for overseas markets, where it had always sold well.

Cherokee sales continued to grow and the Chief model in particular was hot. It seemed everybody wanted one and the waiting list to get one was long. Power steering and power disc brakes were standard on the Chief, along with a fuel tank skid plate. All Cherokees got

new frames, shocks, and springs. Also new was a passenger-side forward-pivoting front bucket seat, to make getting in and out of the rear seat easier. The Cherokee's doors were the same width as the Wagoneer four-door. They were interchangeable, so they didn't have the extra width that doors on most two-door vehicles provide.

Jeep trucks received a new frame, springs, and new wheel cover design. Custom and Pioneer models featured Potomac stripe custom-pleated fabric upholstery, and new graphics greatly improved the look of the instrument panel. Midway through the model year, a new package debuted, the J-10 Honcho, which was a sporty appearance package along the lines of the Chief. It included side appliqué panels, white spoke wheels with Tracker A/T tires, and Levi's interior trim.

Jeep Wagoneer, offered once again in standard and Custom models, got an all-new frame with improved springs for a more comfortable ride and greater durability. New wheel covers debuted, along with an optional front stabilizer bar and new seat upholstery.

Jeep's U.S. retail sales for 1976 came in at 107,487 units, a more than 300 percent gain over

During the year, the factory was unable to acquire enough alloy wheels to meet demand for the Renegade, so the Styling Department came up with an additional sport model fitted with regular steel wheels. Called the Super Jeep, it had a wild stripe package and very attractive interior trim. It's not known how many were sold, but few have survived.

A Jeep in its element. This 1973 CJ-5 looks a little plain but actually has a good many options on it, including whitewall tires, full-wheel discs, free-wheeling front hubs, a chrome bumper, a front passenger seat (yes, that was extra cost), a rear seat, a passenger side mirror, and a spare tire cover.

During 1974, Jeep dealers were offered a special limited-production model of the Jeep truck for their own use as a service vehicle and parts-getter. The truck came with a special cap, special paint and stripes, and an American Motors/Jeep corporate logo on the side. It's not known how many of these have survived.

The big product news for 1974 was a new sport utility wagon called the Cherokee. Though based on the Wagoneer two-door body shell, the Cherokee's styling made it look fresh and all new. Here we see members of the Cherokee Nation with two AMC/Jeep executives wearing headdresses. On the left is William V. Luneburg, president, and on the right is Roy D. Chapin Jr., chairman and CEO. The Cherokee people were consulted before the company decided to use the name on its vehicle.

1970, and crossing the 100,000-unit mark for the first time. The company was earning money hand over fist with Jeep, but unfortunately American Motors' passenger car division was losing it even more quickly. Jeep's parent company lost more than $46 million for the year.

The 1977 model year was another hot one for Jeep and the biggest problem AMC had that year was trying to build enough Jeeps to meet demand. Once again, it failed to do so and that was a shame. The company could have sold many more units than they did.

The 1977 Renegade got new white spoke wheels to replace the expensive alloy ones that had always been part of the package. In February came a new limited-edition package for CJs, called the Golden Eagle. It featured a large decal of an eagle on the hood, brown paint with gold side stripes and trim, Levi's upholstery, gold-painted spoke wheels, a roll bar, a tachometer, and a décor group. It was a real standout and buyers flocked to it in droves. CJs could now be ordered with factory air conditioning, front disc brakes, and a tilt steering wheel. The CB radio craze was hot, so Jeeps now offered that as an option too.

Also debuting in February was a new Golden Eagle pickup, and the response from customers was extremely good. Truck sales began to rise as more and more buyers were attracted to the special models designed by AMC stylists.

There was big news in the Cherokee line, with the introduction of a new four-door Cherokee, which could be had as a standard model or as a Cherokee S. The Cherokee four-door was essentially a Wagoneer with different trim, but because of those trim differences and some good marketing, it attracted a completely

different group of buyers than the Wagoneers and added to Jeep's volume.

But AMC was in trouble. By mid-1977 the company was nearing a crossroads, and there was a great deal of bickering among executives over which direction the company should take. One faction, led by vice chairman Bill McNealy, believed that ever-tightening automobile fuel economy regulations would eventually filter down to the truck market, harming Jeep sales, perhaps fatally. He advocated dropping the passenger car line entirely, replacing it with cars provided by Peugeot, while investing all of AMC's product development cash (most of which would need to be borrowed) in a decisive program to field an entirely new line of Jeep vehicles engineered for greatly improved fuel economy. The other faction, led by executive vice president Gerry Meyers, wanted to downsize passenger car operations, revamp the existing car lines without going into a major redesign, and create an alliance with a foreign manufacturer to gain quick access to the kind of passenger car design and technology it would need to remain in the car business. In essence, Meyers wanted to concentrate resources on salvaging the car business. In the end, the board of directors favored Meyers' proposal.

AMC's troubles could be seen clearly in the financial number for 1977. On total sales volume of more than $2.2 billion, the company netted a profit of just $8.2 million. Jeep was propping up the passenger car division, earning about $100 million a year, which offset the $100 million the car division was losing. Net profits were coming essentially from AM General along with AMC's extensive plastics operations, but how long could the situation go on? Sooner or later the passenger car problem would have to be addressed.

Jeep sold 124,843 vehicles in the United States during calendar year 1977, four times what it had sold in 1970. What was most amazing about this was that the company was selling basically the same vehicles that Kaiser Jeep had sold. AMC hadn't created any new-from-the-ground-up vehicles, only trim packages and special models. Actual tooling

Top: Here's the exciting Jeep Renegade for 1974. With sporty good looks, V-8 power, and terrific performance, the Renegade was an extremely popular model and the factory struggled to keep up with demand.

Bottom: This is the 1974 Jeep pickup, wearing handsome two-tone paint. Starting this year Jeep trucks were identified as J-10 (½-ton) and J-20 (¾-ton) models. Within each series, there were various chassis and suspension options. The J-20 offered GVWs up to 8,000 pounds.

Here's a rare photo of a 1975 Jeep CJ-6 model. With its longer wheelbase, the CJ-6 could be used as a small pickup truck, like this half-cab version. Few of these were sold in the United States, but it was a particularly popular model in overseas markets.

The Jeep Wagoneer kept getting better and better as the years went by. The 1975 model featured a sharp new woodgrain side trim option, plus new standard features, including a light group, carpeting, custom seat trim and door panels, custom wheel covers, and woodgrain instrument panel overlay. Wagoneers also got new springs and shocks for a better ride and improved handling, plus an improved power-steering system and an improved defroster.

bills had been small, and really, the only vehicle that had required anything approaching a significant tooling bill was the CJ-7.

International markets were also strong in 1977. In Iran, Jeep held nearly 75 percent of the four-wheel-drive market, while in Venezuela sales were so hot the company decided to undertake a major expansion of production capacity at the local plant. A new joint venture in Egypt was building a factory that could produce 12,000 Jeeps per year.

Jeep didn't really need to introduce any new products for 1978. Sales were so strong the company could easily sell all it could build and still not be able to meet demand. *But that was a management failing*; the fact was that since 1972 company executives had consistently under-estimated U.S. demand for Jeep vehicles. They might crow about the huge sales increases under their leadership, but the truth was that they could have sold many more than they were. Many Jeep dealers struggled just to keep two or three vehicles in stock, there were long waits for sold orders, and there was little in the way of retail discounts. Dealers were begging for more Jeeps. With full inventories and a real sales push, they probably could have sold 30–40 percent more than they were doing. Management was being overly cautious and it had cost Jeep sales and market share.

One thing management did right was introduce a new Wagoneer model for 1978, the ultra-luxurious Wagoneer Limited, the first domestic SUV with leather interior. The new

Limited oozed luxury at every pore. In addition to the standard V-8, automatic transmission, and Quadra-Trac, air conditioning was also standard equipment, as were thick carpeting, leather-trimmed bucket seats, plush door panels, leather-wrapped steering wheel, power steering and brakes, power tailgate window, woodgrain side panels, and much more. It was the most luxurious SUV in the world and a direct descendent of the groundbreaking 1966 Super Wagoneer.

The rugged Jeep trucks got a new trim option that year. Joining the popular Honcho and Golden Eagle was the sporty new 10-4 package. Offered only on the short wheelbase J-10, it included unique bodyside stripping with black accents, big outline white letter tires on spoke wheels, a roll bar, rear step bumper, and a "10-4" decal. The Pioneer package was dropped.

Further evidence of how consumer tastes were influencing the four-wheel-drive market, CJ models were upgraded by the addition of new standard features that included front disc brakes, an ashtray and cigar lighter, passenger assist handle, passenger-side mirror, and H78

fiberglass belted tires. CJs also got a redesigned heater with improved heating to the rear seat area, higher defroster temperature, and a stronger airflow rate.

It was during 1978 that management finally took some steps to cure the many problems AMC was facing. Jeep was the prime beneficiary of those changes, getting a major

Several stripe designs for the 1976 Cherokee Chief were tried out in the design studios prior to production. This particular vehicle has two stripe ideas, one on each side. This was a common practice, since it made it easier to compare the two ideas.

This is the stripe idea chosen for production of the 1976 Cherokee Chief. It's a trifle muted but still very aggressive looking. The spoke wheels and oversize tires were part of the Chief package.

New for 1976 was the CJ-7. Built on a longer wheelbase, its extra length was primarily for passenger comfort as opposed to cargo capacity. It was better-looking than the CJ-6 and sold very well. The plastic top offered greatly improved appearance and performance compared to the CJ-5's steel hardtop.

In the background, brilliant Jeep engineer Roy Lunn and his team were working on a line of all-new senior Jeeps for the 1980s. These vehicles would be noticeably smaller and lighter, yet retain about 90 percent of the big Jeep's interior roominess while delivering world-class fuel efficiency and greatly improved ride, handling, and capability. Lunn was testing a new type of full-time four-wheel drive and a radical new transfer case designed by Fergusson in Great Britain. He was excited because it offered greatly improved smoothness, silence, and efficiency, along with superior traction control.

In October 1978, Gerry Meyers became chairman of AMC. Earlier the company had begun discussions with French automaker Peugeot about distributing their cars through the AMC network. It wasn't quite the deal Meyers wanted. His idea was to form a pact to build European-designed cars in his Kenosha passenger car plant. His dealers couldn't survive selling only Jeep vehicles; they had to have more sales volume to cover costs. At the very least a deal with Peugeot would provide

increase in production capacity beginning in September when the American Motors factory in Brampton, Ontario, was converted from building passenger cars to building Jeep CJs. It was a bold move and a smart one. In one stroke AMC reduced its passenger car capacity—of which it had way too much—by 50,000 units while increasing its Jeep output—of which it had too little—by the same amount. Jeep dealers would at last be able to look forward to having nearly as many CJs as there was demand for.

A popular model in the Cherokee line was this Cherokee S, which added many comfort and luxury items to the standard equipment list, including the side stripes and alloy wheels seen here.

his dealers with another product to sell and might eventually lead to Peugeot-designed cars being built in America. But then, literally hours before he was to sign the Peugeot deal, another French automaker, Renault, called to ask if they could submit a proposal more along the lines that Meyers was looking for. Since he was not fully satisfied with Peugeot as a partner—he later said the French executives looked down on AMC with disdain—Meyers decided to enter talks with Renault about selling their cars through his distribution network in America, while gaining access to Renault front-drive components and engines that could be used in a

new generation of AMC cars. In addition, Renault had an excellent diesel engine that could be used in Jeep vehicles at some point in the future. Going with Renault had the potential to work out better than the Peugeot deal, so that was set aside and negotiations with Renault commenced.

By the last quarter of 1978, the beginning of an AMC turnaround was clearly demonstrated when a fiscal year profit of $36.6 million was reported on gross dollar sales of $2.58 billion worldwide. It wasn't the level of profitability the company needed to survive long term, but at least American Motors, and thus Jeep, was heading in the right direction. Still, there was plenty to worry about. The *only* thing keeping AMC from bankruptcy was Jeep. If its sales began to fall, what then?

As the year came to a close, Meyers was interviewed by the industry magazine *Ward's Auto World*. When the reporter remarked that some people were saying that the four-wheel-drive market was about to peak, Meyers replied, "Baloney, absolute baloney." He seemed confident the growth would go on indefinitely. It may have been wishful thinking, because for Meyers and AMC, the thought of the market peaking was too unpleasant to even consider.

Jeeps were selling like crazy in 1977, and the factory again struggled to keep up with orders. This year, Renegade got new white spoke wheels to replace the expensive alloy ones that had always been part of the package. CJs could now be ordered with factory air conditioning, front disc brakes, and a tilt steering wheel.

The 1977 Jeep lineup was strong, and sales of heavily equipped models were particularly good, as consumers expressed their desire for more luxurious SUVs. Cherokee now offered a four-door version, as seen here.

During July 1978, Jeep model year production in the United States topped the 150,000th level, marking the highest production in Jeep Corporation history. The landmark vehicle was a red CJ-7 Renegade, shown here being driven off the line by Ohio Governor James A. Rhodes with AMC president Gerry Meyers in the passenger seat.

For the 1979 model year, Jeep offered mostly improvements and refinements to its existing vehicles. The Wagoneer Limited now included a choice of AM/FM/eight-track or AM/FM/CB radio as standard equipment. One-piece aluminum bumpers were new, as was an elegant new grille and rectangular headlights. The standard tires in 1979 were American Eagle Flexten WSW radials.

Jeep trucks also got the new one-piece front bumper along with a sharp new grille, rectangular headlights, and a new custom steering wheel.

Cherokee now offered the popular Golden Eagle package in addition to the S and Chief packages. The Golden Eagle, like the Chief, was available only on the wide-wheel two-door model, while the S could be had on any Cherokee. The year's Cherokees received the new one-piece bumpers, a new grille, rectangular headlights, plus a new custom four-spoke steering wheel. New options in 1979 included a lighted visor vanity mirror, extra quiet insulation package, smooth ride suspension (except on wide-wheel models), and intermittent windshield wipers.

CJ models also saw enhancements, which included a new soft top with better fit, greater strength, and better leak resistance. The 258-cid six was now standard equipment, and the 304 V-8 remained an option. As before, a four-speed transmission with a very low "granny" first gear was an option for people who tended to use their vehicles for extreme off-roading or for plowing.

In January 1979, Gerry Meyers announced

the new agreement whereby AMC would take over sales of Renault cars in the United States and Canada, while Renault would begin selling Jeeps in Columbia and France. It sounded like a good idea, but it was destined to play out much differently from Meyer's plan.

There was a new limited-production CJ-5 debuting in mid-1979. Marking the 25th anniversary of the start of CJ-5 production in late 1954, a special Silver Anniversary CJ-5 was introduced in the spring. It featured special Quick Silver metallic paint—the vehicles were produced at the Canadian facility because Toledo reportedly couldn't paint that color—and included special Renegade stripes in silver tones, black vinyl bucket seats with silver trim, chrome 15x8 wheels, white-letter tires, and an instrument panel badge. The model quickly sold out.

It was decided that a large new paint facility would be constructed at the main Jeep plant in Toledo to eliminate a major bottleneck, providing a 50 percent increase in Jeep production by 1981. But Jeep dealers needed more vehicles right now, so in February 1979 Gerry Meyers announced that AMC had a plan that would quickly increase production of Jeep Cherokee and Wagoneer four-door models by about 50,000 units. In a surprising change, the new increase would

come from the company's Kenosha, Wisconsin, passenger car plants. A portion of the huge facility would be converted to Jeep production, which would cost $30 million but could go online in less than a year. At the current rate of demand, that production was badly needed. The ultimate goal was total Jeep production capacity of 350,000 units within three years. Separately, the small plant in Venezuela announced it would double Jeep production to 14,000 units annually.

But something happened in June 1979; the market for four-wheel-drive vehicles slumped to an annual rate of 700,000. It had been running at about a million units per year. In July, the annual rate rose to 830,000 units, an improvement but still well off the high point. Fuel economy was the main problem. In early 1979, the Shah of Iran had been forced to flee his country amid massive protests. The fiery anti-American Muslim cleric Ayatollah Khomeini soon became Iran's de facto leader and during the chaos oil production plummeted, setting off a panic that drove up prices. Suddenly there were long lines and fistfights at gas stations—just as there had been

This is a landmark vehicle as well: the 1978 Jeep Wagoneer Limited, the most luxurious four-wheel-drive vehicle on the market. Sales of this high-priced unit would be even better than the loftiest predictions and would do so for years to come. Today these are highly desirable collector vehicles.

The Jeep assembly lines were humming in 1979, as can be seen in this photo taken on the CJ line; however, world events during the year would trigger a sharp recession that would drastically change the four-wheel-drive market.

Top: To celebrate 25 years of the Jeep CJ-5, the company created this 1979 Jeep Silver Anniversary CJ-5, which was a specially trimmed and painted CJ-5 Renegade. The paint was a special shade exclusive to this model, as was the stripe package and interior seat material. The vehicle came shod with chrome wheels and Goodyear Tracker AT tires.

Bottom: In response to slowing sales, Jeep introduced two new limited-edition models for 1980: the CJ Golden Hawk and the Cherokee Golden Hawk. The CJ Golden Hawk package could be ordered on the CJ-5 and CJ-7 soft top models or the CJ-7 hardtop. The Cherokee was only available on the two-door wide-wheel model. Each included a long list of special interior and exterior trim. Not many were sold and it's not known if any have survived.

in 1974—and the economy began to contract. Jeep had a small assembly plant in Iran, which the locals were eager to keep open, but American stevedores soon refused to load outgoing ships with the necessary Jeep parts kits that the plant assembled.

Up to that point the fact that Jeep vehicles—all four-wheel-drive vehicles for that matter—got relatively poor gas mileage hadn't been a big concern to the public. They might complain about it, but they loved their big vehicles so much that they tended to overlook the problem. Anyway, gas prices over the years were not all that bad and, of course, there hadn't been a problem with availability for some time. Now, however, people were holding off purchasing an SUV or going with a more fuel-efficient vehicle. In response to slowing sales, Jeep launched a special $99 soft top promotion for CJs and a rebate program for Cherokees and trucks equipped with Quadra-Trac. It helped, for a while.

Of course, some AMC top executives had predicted that poor fuel economy would become a problem, albeit under a different scenario, and that problem was now unfolding. Thankfully, Jeep dealers had a huge backlog of sold orders that would be months in arriving, and they were anxious to finally be able to

build up their inventory, so the downturn didn't hurt Jeep Corporation much during the 1979 fiscal year, which, as always, ended September 30. The downward trend could be spotted in the nine-month report to the stockholders, which noted that Jeep sales in the third quarter actually declined for the first time in quite a while. Although the drop was by less than 500 units, that was an ominous portent because up to that point sales had been running up to 45 percent over the prior year. The company also noted that in July it had actually reduced production of Cherokee and Wagoneer models. Clearly, something was happening to the market.

As noted, the downturn in four-wheel-drive sales didn't have a dramatic effect on American Motors' fiscal year ending September 30, 1979. Total sales volume topped the $3 billion mark for the first time, and net profits just shy of $84 million were reported—AMC's best year ever. During the fiscal year, the company sold its dealers 207,642 Jeeps, outselling cars for the first time ever, albeit by less than 100 units. It was a tremendous year for the company. Unfortunately, it would be several years before AMC again made a profit, let alone a record one, and in the meantime Jeep and its parent would face the very real danger of simply going out of business.

Here we see another popular package Jeep, the 1979 J-10 truck with the optional "10-4" appearance package.

The 1980 model year opened early—in late August 1979—probably because Jeep had so much new to offer. Two goals were targeted: improving fuel economy and increasing the luxury and capability aspects of Jeep vehicles.

In a major move to offer class-leading fuel economy, Jeep introduced a new standard engine for CJs, called the "Hurricane," a modern four-cylinder engine originally dubbed the "Iron Duke" and purchased from GM. The company didn't advertise its 82-horsepower rating, perhaps worried that buyers would be turned off by the low power. But with the new standard transmission, a regular four-speed that offered evenly spaced gear ratios, the net effect was adequate power and surprisingly good fuel economy. Also included was a new,

lighter weight transfer case. The four-cylinder CJ received an EPA rating of 21 miles per gallon in the city and 27 on the highway, which was the highest rating for a conventional four-wheel-drive vehicle in America. To further improve fuel economy, CJs with automatic transmissions now came with part-time four-wheel drive rather than the more fuel-thirsty full-time system. Free-wheeling hubs were made standard equipment, which also increased real-world fuel economy.

Cherokee, Wagoneer, and truck models received a new Quadra-Trac full-time four-wheel-drive system that was lighter and offered improved performance, plus better fuel economy. It featured a viscous coupling for smoother, quieter operation and came standard with both high and low ranges. It was standard equipment on Wagoneer and optional on Cherokee and truck models, which also offered an optional automatic transmission and part-time four-wheel-drive option. Cherokees and trucks came standard with a manual four-speed gearbox.

Also new for 1980 was the Laredo trim option. On CJs this included a chrome grille overlay, chrome wheels, Wrangler 9Rx15 radial tires, special striping, and high back bucket seats. It was a beautiful package, the most luxurious CJ ever

Here's the Wagoneer Custom for 1981 with optional two-tone paint. This year all senior Jeeps got new springs to reduce ride height and wind drag. In addition, they got a new front air dam to funnel air downward for less wind resistance and new drag-free disc brakes.

This photo taken inside the Jeep styling studios is undated. It shows a CJ-7 called the Iron Duke. Was this planned to be a special model carrying the four-cylinder GM engine?

One of the most famous Jeep ads of all time is this one depicting a cowboy and his mount, a CJ-5 Laredo, rightly referred to as a legend. Jeep was building some of the best vehicles ever during this period, but the economy was poor and sales were lagging.

built to that point. Soft top CJ-7s could now be ordered with steel doors with wind-up windows.

In addition to its new four-speed transmission, Cherokee also got a new lightweight part-time four-wheel-drive transfer case that was more efficient. It, too, offered a Laredo package on the wide-wheel model, which came with 10Rx15 Wrangler radial tires on chrome wheels, unique bucket seats and door trim, luxury carpeting, special striping, and a sports steering wheel. The S, Chief, and Golden Eagle packages remained available. Power windows and locks were new luxury options.

For the first time in seven years, the Wagoneer was available with an optional automatic transmission and part-time four-wheel-drive system, or with the new, more-efficient Quadra-Trac four-wheel drive, which was standard equipment. A four-speed manual transmission was also offered. The 258-cid six-cylinder engine was now available on all Wagoneers as a delete option in place of the standard V-8. Power windows and door locks were now standard on the Limited.

Jeep trucks got the new transfer case and transmission technologies the other senior Jeeps offered, and likewise got the new Laredo

package as a new option. There was a new model as well, the Sportside, which boasted an old-style step side body with fiberglass "balloon" rear fenders. The Sportside came only as a Custom or Honcho model, and standard equipment included white spoke wheels with big 15x8 Tracker A/T tires.

Sales held up fairly well in the first quarter of 1980, with car sales increasing enough to offset lower Jeep sales. The quarter's profit dropped to $12.8 million, from $18.9, but in light of the worsening recession that was certainly acceptable. New president Paul Tippet said AMC management was ". . . reasonably pleased with our performance" and predicted the company would remain profitable through the year.

But Tippett was quite wrong. For the 12 months ending September 30, 1980, wholesale sales of Jeep vehicles in the United States and Canada—that is, sales to its dealers—fell by nearly 98,000 units, while sales of less-profitable passenger cars grew by only about 31,000 units. But the pain goes beyond just the number of vehicles sold. The fact was that in order to generate even those poor numbers the company had to launch expensive marketing and rebate

Jeep Scrambler SR Sport

In mid-1981 Jeep unveiled the new Scrambler, a mini-pickup based on a stretched CJ-7 platform. The Scrambler was sporty and attractive, but Jeep did a poor selling job with it. Today these vehicles are highly prized by collectors.

programs that burned up a lot of its cash and ruined any chance at profitability. In the end, the company reported a net loss of $159.7 million, an incredible figure for that period. But that year, by coincidence, management had decided to change AMC's fiscal year to run January 1 to December 31, same as its domestic competitors, and on that basis, the losses swelled to more than $208 million. It was an unmitigated disaster for a company the size of AMC. And it was by no means going to be a one-year occurrence. The auto market was in a slump that was worsening each day. The planned $30 million investment in bringing Jeep production to Kenosha was canceled. It was time to slash Jeep capacity, not grow it.

Faced with worsening sales, Gerry Meyers bowed to the inevitable and announced in November 1980 that AMC would spend $1 billion developing new car and Jeep models. The all-new Jeeps, which Roy Lunn was already working on, would begin to appear toward the end of 1983, the new cars a year earlier than that. In retrospect, he probably should have

tried to bring the new Jeeps out first. To get the money needed for such an expensive program, Renault upped its stake in AMC to 46 percent, giving it de facto control of the company. Management said that Renault would not dictate to AMC, but how long did they really expect that arrangement to last?

Meanwhile, the 1981 Jeep models were announced. There were a great many engineering changes that year, all of them to further improve Jeep's fuel economy. The biggest change was in the 258-cid six-cylinder engine. It was completely redesigned with a lighter, thinner block, with greater use of aluminum and plastic parts. The new engine was more durable, offered greater smoothness and better fuel economy, and weighed 90 pounds less than before. It was available as standard or optional equipment on all Jeep vehicles. All 1981 Jeeps benefited from greater use of one- and two-sided galvanized steel for better corrosion protection.

All senior Jeeps got new springs to reduce ride height and thereby reduce wind drag. In addition, they got a new front air dam to funnel air downward, for less wind resistance. Jeep trucks also received a new roof panel that eliminated the lip over the windshield, again for better aerodynamics. Senior Jeeps also got new drag-free disc brakes, along with radial tires on all models with standard-size tires.

In March 1981 Jeep added an interesting new model to its lineup, the Scrambler pickup. Based on a long wheelbase version of the CJ-7, the new truck was compact, fuel efficient, and very attractive. But Jeep fumbled the merchandising of the Scrambler, advertising it as a sport utility that could also carry things rather than what it was: a small, four-wheel-drive truck from the best name in four-wheel-drive vehicles. The base Scrambler was an open roadster; to turn it into a pickup truck one had to order either a cab-style soft top or a removable plastic hardtop. With Jeep versatility and 27 miles per gallon highway fuel economy, it should have sold better than it did.

In August a new Jeep assembly plant opened in Brisbane, Australia, to assemble Jeep Cherokee and truck models for the local market. CJs for Australia continued to be imported from the United States.

Cherokee added two new models for 1981, four-door versions of the Chief and Laredo. The S models were dropped. Wagoneer added a new midrange Brougham model to its existing Custom and Limited offerings.

CJ-5 and CJ-7 returned for 1981 with not much different, though they did offer the new lightweight six as an option. EPA fuel economy numbers for the four were 22 city and 27 highway, really excellent considering the CJs were still the same sturdy vehicles they'd always been. The six was rated at 17 city and 24 highway. Adding the automatic transmission yielded much lower results.

But neither the new models nor the improved fuel economy was enough to move

A very special Jeep was created for 1982, the limited-edition CJ-7 Jamboree. Built to celebrate the 30th anniversary of the Jeep Jamboree off-road event, the Jamboree included special Topaz Gold paint, chrome wheels and bumpers, a Ramsey electric winch, and a whole lot more. Only 2,500 of these vehicles were produced.

Perhaps the most important project in AMC history was the development of the all-new Jeep Cherokee XJ series for 1984. This photo, probably from around 1979–80, shows a mockup of one proposal. Although it looks similar to the production model, it varies in most details.

the needle for Jeep in 1981, with U.S. retail sales totals for the calendar year plummeting to 63,275 units, though oddly enough, sales of Wagoneer actually increased by 20 percent. Passenger car retail sales fell slightly, too, as the economy continued to contract. In this environment, AMC lost $138.8 million, a $70 million improvement over 1980 but a huge loss nonetheless. By January 1982 Gerry Meyers, the man who brought Renault into the AMC fold, was out the door. His replacement as chairman was Paul Tippet, with Renault executive Jose Deduerwaerder as president and COO.

For the 1982 model year, there were further improvements to the Jeep line. A new five-speed overdrive manual transmission became available on most models, boosting highway fuel economy substantially. Also debuting on senior Jeeps was the new Selec-Trac four-wheel-drive system, which combined the many benefits of full-time four-wheel drive with the ability to switch into two-wheel drive for better fuel economy. Selec-Trac replaced Quadra-Trac and was available only in combination with an automatic transmission.

Senior models were now rated at a credible 18 miles per gallon city and 25 highway, while four-cylinder CJs were rated at 23 miles per gallon city and 28 highway, both a real achievement that would have brought in thousands more buyers if only the economy wasn't in such bad shape. Inflation had become a big problem as well, with vehicle prices rising almost on a quarterly basis and a new term, "sticker shock," becoming well established in consumer's minds.

The 1982 Jeep pickup line got an all-new Pioneer package, which included the basic goodies from the Custom package, for example, deluxe grain vinyl bench seat, bright door and window moldings, Deluxe door trim panels,

Here is the same vehicle as seen from the front; the differences are more obvious. The fender, hood, grille, and bumpers are all different from the production job, as are the rear quarters and roof.

American Motors didn't have a suitable location for outdoor viewing of prototypes and mockups. Famed Jeep designer Bob Nixon once described it as a "rat-infested slab of concrete in the trash area where we displayed our fiberglass models to AMC upper management." Here we see an advanced mockup of the proposed new Cherokee.

instrument cluster trim, hood insulation and passenger assist handle, and added an upper bodyside scuff molding, tailgate stripes, Western Weave cloth and vinyl bench seat upholstery with matching door trim panels, sports steering wheel, painted rear step bumper, full wheel covers, extra-quiet insulation, and more. The year brought the introduction of an entirely new concept for Jeep, the CJ-7 Limited, with

luxury heretofore unseen in a CJ vehicle. The Limited came standard with power steering and power brakes, AM/FM radio, monochromatic paint with a color-keyed hardtop and wheel lip extensions, bodyside stripes, chrome front bumper and rear bumperettes, bodyside steps, black-painted windshield and window frames, dual outside mirrors, color-keyed spoke wheels with bright trim rings, P235/75R15 Goodyear Arriva radial tires, a special improved ride package that included softer springs and shocks, special high back bucket seats in Western Weave cloth or optional leather, special sound insulation, and much, much more, all designed to bring the luxury of a full-size vehicle into a smaller, more fuel-efficient package. It was like no CJ ever built, before or since. In response to reduced demand, the V-8 engine was no longer offered in CJs.

All 1982 Jeeps built in Toledo had their exterior paint applied in the all-new paint facility that was authorized back when there was an urgent need to build more Jeeps. Jeep paint quality—always a weak point—was now dramatically better.

A fiberglass mockup, circa 1980–81, gets closer to the production shape. Look just past the windshield and you'll see a Range Rover, likely bought as a comparison vehicle.

In this frontal design we count 14 slots in the grille, a bit too many for comfort. Thankfully this idea was rejected.

January 1982 brought another new limited-edition Jeep, the CJ-7 Jamboree, created to celebrate the 30th anniversary of the Jeepers Jamboree, an annual off-road event for hardcore four-wheel-drive enthusiasts. The Jamboree offered special hood lettering, special Gold Topaz paint, chrome-styled wheels, chrome front bumper and rear bumperettes, a black vinyl soft top, high-back bucket seats in black vinyl, center console, black carpeting, and an instrument panel numbered ID plaque. Required options included the 258-cid six, five-speed transmission, power steering and brakes, Trac-Loc rear differential, and a few other items.

In May 1982, Renault finally, and reluctantly, began selling Jeeps in France, Belgium, and Luxembourg. The model selected for sale was a CJ-7 powered by a 2.0-liter four-cylinder Renault gas or diesel engine, hooked up to a Renault gearbox. Only a few thousand were expected to be sold annually, but that was many times more than had formerly been sold there. In the previous four years, only 173 CJ-7s had been sold in France.

For fiscal 1982 it was the same story as the prior two years. American Motors reported a huge loss, this time $153 million. But there was a glimmer of hope in those numbers. In the fourth quarter, the company lost only $2.9 million, a big improvement. For the year Jeep sales grew by about 4,000 units in the United States and Canada, but dropped by 18,000 units in overseas markets as the economic woes spread around the world.

The number of CJ-5 variations for 1983 was cut because this was the final year of U.S. production for the venerated model. Only the base and Renegade versions were offered and only with the 258-cid six. The CJ-7 still came standard with a four, and offered Renegade,

This Cherokee prototype was photographed at Meadowbrook Hall in May 1981, at which time the final design was locked in, except for minor trim details.

Laredo, and Limited versions. The Cherokee line also was trimmed, with narrow-wheel two doors available only in Base and Pioneer models, while the four-door was offered only as a Pioneer. The wide-wheel two-door was offered for the Chief and Laredo models, but no base model. In the Wagoneer line, the Custom model was dropped, so only the Brougham and Limited were available.

All this model trimming to simplify the lineup was necessary because by the fourth quarter the long-awaited new Jeep XJ models—downsized Cherokee and Wagoneer—were finally going into production. There would be many changes then.

During the year, Jeep announced a new joint venture in China, in which it would own 31.6 percent of a new company called Beijing Jeep Corporation. The new unit was the largest joint venture in China at the time and the first time an American vehicle would be produced in that country since before World War II. It was expected to become the largest Jeep operation outside of North America, and it was hoped the new company would export Jeeps to other Asian countries, especially Japan. Not all of its goals would be reached.

For 1983 AMC once again lost a ton of money, more than $146 million. But there was light on the horizon: sales of Jeep vehicles soared in the fourth quarter and for the year were up nearly 23,000 units worldwide. The reason? The new 1984 XJs were introduced and they were taking the market by storm.

It needs to be said: The 1984 Jeep XJ Cherokee and Wagoneer, the most completely redesigned Jeeps since 1963, were the most advanced four-wheel-drive vehicles in the world. Everything about them was new, and they introduced more new technology to the SUV market than any vehicle before or since.

The new Jeeps were noticeably smaller, 21 inches shorter in overall length, and weighed about 1,200 pounds less than the full-size Cherokee and Wagoneer yet retained 90 percent of their interior room. The lighter weight meant they could be powered by the new AMC 2.5-liter four-cylinder engine, which would provide superior fuel economy and adequate power. The Cherokee with a four-cylinder engine and stick transmission was rated at 24 miles per gallon city and 33 miles per gallon highway. That was as good as many economy cars. A GM-sourced V-6 was optional.

Although 6 inches narrower than before, the new Jeeps were 2 inches wider than Chevy Blazer, 4 inches wider than the Ford Bronco II, and offered more interior space than either of

Here's an interesting, never-seen-before proposal for the upcoming Jeep Wrangler. In this September 1982 mockup, the Jeep has a much more exaggerated bend in the grille. Don't reject it out of hand; the look grows on you.

them. The new Jeeps held five passengers, not four like the competition. Jeep's innovative pedestal mounted front seats allowed greater rear seat foot room.

In engineering the XJ Jeeps, Roy Lunn and his team came up with a new type of frame called the Uniframe. Essentially it was a robust stamped-steel frame welded to the underside of a strong unit-body structure, giving the strength of a conventional heavy frame with the weight advantages of Unibody construction. This was one of the keys to the new Jeep's low weight and sturdiness. It also greatly improved on-road ride and handling, while lowering the ride height without compromising critical ground clearance. Uniframe was a major advance in SUV design.

So was the Quadra-Link front suspension, which utilized a solid front axle for superior

The new Cherokee and Wagoneer XJ models finally arrived for the 1984 model year and were an instant hit. For the first time in history, all three leading off-road magazines picked the same vehicle as "4x4 of the Year": the Jeep Cherokee. It was not the last time a Jeep would be a Triple Crown winner.

To appease buyers who still wanted a full-size Jeep but couldn't afford a Grand Wagoneer, Jeep rolled out this 1984 Custom Wagoneer equipped with automatic transmission, two-speed part-time four-wheel drive with free-wheeling hubs, air conditioning, Custom interior trim, and more—all at the bargain price of $15,995. Not many people were interested in it; the Grand Wagoneer far outsold the Custom.

In a surprising move during 1985, Jeep added two-wheel-drive versions of the Cherokee to appeal to people living in warmer climates that didn't call for four-wheel drive.

strength yet provided the ride and handling qualities of an independent front suspension. The new Jeeps offered shift-on-the-fly part-time four-wheel drive or Jeep's exclusive Selec-Trac four-wheel drive.

The new Jeeps were amazing; they had the highest dynamic ground clearance in their class, yet also had the lowest step-in height. They were faster than the competition, got better gas mileage, boasted a 4,200-pound towing capacity, and had a longer wheelbase for better ride and comfort.

Styling was outstanding. A team led by Bob Nixon created an all-new look that was like no Jeep before it, yet was instantly recognizable as a Jeep—an amazing accomplishment. In clinics it outscored every outside proposal that was shown and virtually blew them away. The XJ

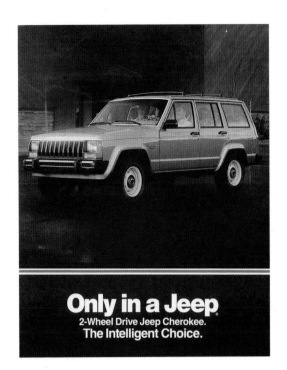

Only in a Jeep
2-Wheel Drive Jeep Cherokee.
The Intelligent Choice.

The downsized Wagoneer XJ was right-sized and luxurious enough for anyone. This is the 1985 model. Note the rich grille, stylish alloy wheels, and woodgrain accent panels.

4WD LIVING IN THE LUXURY LANE.

JEEP WAGONEER LIMITED. Luxury choice number one from Jeep is the elegant 5-passenger, 4-door Wagoneer Limited with shift-on-the-fly 2WD/4WD Selec-Trac, leather-trimmed seats, choice of standard 2.5L, 4-cylinder engine, optional V-6, or new 2.1L turbo diesel power-plant, plus standard features you'd expect to find on fine luxury wagons.

25 EST HWY **21** EPA EST MPG

Use these figures for comparison. Your results may differ due to driving speed, weather condition and trip length. Actual highway mileage may be lower.

would go on to become one of the most iconic Jeeps of all time.

The new Jeeps were well-priced, too, with the four-wheel-drive Cherokee two-door starting at just $9,995. Jeep offered the greatest range of models in the industry. Dealer orders were off the charts, because everyone recognized that Jeep had created the product of the decade. *Motor Trend* magazine said it best: "Today's XJ-series represent such an advancement over the previous vehicles that there's little point in even talking about comparisons." The new XJ Jeeps were named "4x4 Vehicle of the Year" by all three leading off-road magazines. No other

vehicle had ever earned that "Triple Crown" distinction. Overnight they became the new benchmark in four-wheel-drive vehicles.

The old Cherokee was dropped, while the former Wagoneer Limited was renamed Grand Wagoneer and remained in the lineup. And, in case someone still wanted a full-size Jeep that wasn't as loaded (or expensive) as the Grand Wagoneer, a Custom Wagoneer was offered for a short time, with automatic transmission, part-time four-wheel drive, custom interior trim, and air conditioning. Not many were sold. The rest of the 1984 Jeep line was mainly carryover.

For fiscal 1984 Jeep wholesale sales to dealers nearly doubled, to 171,036 in the United States and Canada. Overseas sales climbed 10 percent to 22,392. Retail sales in the United States alone were more than 150,000 units, so Jeep clearly was on the comeback trail. AMC actually earned a profit, though only $15 million.

The 1985 Jeep line offered new features to excite buyers. Cherokee and Wagoneer now offered a Renault-built Turbo-Diesel engine good for 29 miles per gallon city or highway. More impressive was the addition of "shift-on-the-fly" capability to

By 1985 the Jeep plant in Toledo, Ohio, was running flat out to keep up with demand for the new Jeep vehicles, a far cry from just a few years earlier when things looked grim.

In this photo we see a "what if?" design. What if we turned a Cherokee XJ into a four-door sedan? How would it look? Actually, it looks very handsome, much like the concurrent Volvo sedans, which were about the same size as the Jeep.

the Selec-Trac full-time four-wheel-drive system. Cherokee added a new Laredo trim option.

The big Grand Wagoneer—the most coveted SUV in the world—also got "shift-on-the-fly" capability, along with a fold-up feature for the center armrest so it could be used to expand the front seat to hold three people (a third front seat belt was also provided). A new suspension system provided a smoother, quieter ride. CJ-7, Scrambler, and truck models received minor refinements.

Midyear brought a new line of two-wheel-drive Cherokees added to the model mix in order to grab a bigger share of the southern U.S. market, where four-wheel drive was less popular. The base price was $9,195 for the two-door Cherokee two-wheeler.

In January 1985 AMC president Jose Dedeurwaerder unveiled a new Comanche compact pickup, based on the Cherokee. It was a sharp-looking truck and would go into production in the fall for the 1986 model year.

Worldwide Jeep wholesale sales to dealers in fiscal 1985 soared to a record-setting 240,288 units, an amazing 192,835 just in the United States and Canada. It was a miraculous recovery and solid testimony to the excellence of the Jeep XJ series, and the continuing popularity of the CJ and Grand Wagoneer. Still, the company reported a huge loss of $125 million because sales of its Renault passenger cars had fallen off dramatically.

The 1986 model year started off with a bang. The all-new Comanche pickup was introduced and was an immediate hit with buyers. Comanche was offered initially only as a long bed model, but that didn't restrict sales too badly. The Scrambler pickup, which never met its sales

Still pretty after all these years, the Jeep CJ-7 offered a lot of fun and capability in a tight, well-developed package. This is a 1986 model with optional chrome wheel and outline white letter tires.

expectations, was dropped, leaving the CJ-7 as the sole offering in the CJ line. Cherokee and Wagoneer received a fuel-injected version of the four-cylinder engine as standard equipment, giving them more power, greater smoothness, and improved fuel economy as well. Cherokee also now offered a special Off-Road package for serious off-roaders, with heavy-duty springs and shocks and a slight lift to the body. Wagoneer got controversial new front-end styling with quad rectangular headlamps, while the Grand Wagoneer received a new grille and stand-up hood ornament—obligatory for luxury vehicles in that decade.

But November 1985 brought an announcement that was a rear shocker. After 40 years of CJ production, the 1986 model year would be the last. Jeep would cease building the CJ-7 that January.

Worried Jeep enthusiasts soon learned that the venerable CJ was being replaced by an all-

new sport utility called the Wrangler. At first glance it appeared to be simply an updated CJ-7, but it was completely new. Designed to offer more comfort and features than the CJ-7, Wrangler came standard with a tighter, better-fitting soft top and steel doors, a fuel-injected four-cylinder engine, five-speed manual transmission, one-piece rear-tire swing-away tailgate, and more. Wrangler's suspension was based on lessons learned when designing the XJ Jeeps and was smoother riding without giving up any of its off-road capability. Wrangler was considered an early 1987 model. In Canada it was called the YJ because the Wrangler name was already trademarked there.

Reaction to the new Wrangler was mixed. While most enthusiasts appreciated the big improvements in ride, handling, and off-road capability, they didn't like the styling, specifically the Wrangler's bent grille and

The best-looking compact pickup truck on the market in 1986 was the Jeep Comanche, shown here with optional X sport package. It was the first true Unibody conventional pickup and was a rugged, solidly built machine. These trucks are surprisingly popular today.

Jeep Wagoneer was given a facelift for 1986, with stacked quad headlamps and a split grille. The look wasn't as popular as the original, however.

square headlights. Some Jeep enthusiasts began wearing t-shirts that proclaimed "Real Jeeps Have Round Headlamps."

Meanwhile, there was another management change. AMC's new president, Joseph Cappy, was busy trying to stem the losses in the passenger car division while also addressing the systemic problems at Jeep. The Toledo plant had become unattractive because of high labor cost, extremely inefficient work practices, a militant union, and an outdated facility. The Toledo union was the only one of the 26 locals Cappy dealt with that had refused to accept a stretch-out on repayment of deferred benefits agreed upon in an earlier deal, and this was costing AMC a fortune when it could least afford it. An angry Cappy talked openly about the unthinkable: moving Jeep production out of Toledo and into a modern plant in some other state, most likely in the South, where union activities were almost nonexistent. Various states were offering enticing incentives to move production there. The Japanese automakers were moving to the South in force; why not do

the same with Jeep? It would boost profitability by a large amount.

One thing the company was silent on was a program to come up with a new product, a Jeep smaller than anything heretofore done. Called the JJ, for Junior Jeep, as it was originally envisioned it would be a small four-wheel drive similar to the Suzuki Samurai that had recently come onto the U.S. market at a price of just $6,200, some $1,500 less than the most basic CJ and close to $3,000 less than the upcoming Wrangler. More than 47,000 Suzukis were sold

Meanwhile, the Grand Wagoneer continued to sell a steady number of profitable vehicles. The big Grand was the most admired four-wheel-drive vehicle on the planet.

in the United States in 1986, more than 83,000 in 1987. Clearly, something had to be done.

In a market thick with competition and rampant price-cutting, Jeep sales fell by 19,000 units in 1986, while car sales dropped by about 85,000 units, and AMC lost money once again, some $91 million this time. Swirling about in the background were rumors that Jeep was about to be sold to another company. Chrysler was believed to be the most likely buyer.

Jeep unveiled a new budget-minded model for 1987, the two-wheel-drive Comanche Sportruck. A short bed pickup with impressive standard equipment that included the most powerful engine in its class, Sportruck was a bargain at just $6,495.

There was an exciting new Cherokee model that year, the Cherokee Limited, which provided buyers with a high level of standard equipment along with distinctive styling touches to create the most luxurious Cherokee ever. Cherokee Limited was a four-door Cherokee with color-keyed fender flares, front air dam, headlights bezels, bumpers, and grille. Rear side windows and tailgate glass were deep-tinted glass. On the inside was a gorgeous leather interior with wingback bucket seats with six-way power adjustment, air conditioning, power steering, brakes, windows, locks, mirrors and antenna, tilt wheel, and too much more to list. A four-speed automatic transmission was standard equipment as well. Response was overwhelming and in an odd twist Cherokee Limited became one of the most-stolen cars in the country. Everybody wanted one.

Even bigger news for 1987, though, was the new optional 4.0 six-cylinder engine available on all Comanche, Cherokee, and Wagoneer models. Developed by AMC engineers and based on the previous AMC six, the new 4.0 boasted fuel injection and 173 horsepower,

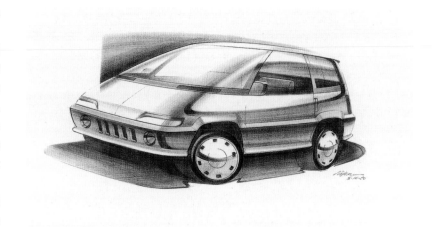

by far the most powerful engine in its class. A Cherokee could now accelerate 0 to 60 in 9.5 seconds. With it, Jeep could outrun any compact SUV or pickup on the market with ease. Overnight, Jeep became the performance leader in the compact SUV market. Just as important, it meant that now all Jeep vehicles would be powered by engines produced in-house, which would greatly reduce costs. A new four-speed automatic transmission also debuted. The GM V-6 formerly used was dropped.

March 1987 brought shocking news. The rumors were true: AMC was being sold to Chrysler Corporation. In a deal Chrysler chairman Lee Iacocca cut with Renault, the number three American automaker bought the number four and quickly dropped the American Motors name. Chrysler didn't want AMC or its cars; the prize in the package was Jeep, and Chrysler got it at a low price—less than $2 billion for what Iacocca called "the best-known automotive brand name in the world."

The purchase price was estimated at $1.1 billion, but Chrysler was also taking on all of AMC's debt and pension obligations, so the numbers can be interpreted many ways. But

Anticipating future products, legendary Jeep designer Bob Nixon created this Jeep Skate, a concept for a four-wheel-drive minivan that could hold five passengers. This sketch is dated August 10, 1986.

For 1987 Jeep offered a base model Comanche that was well-equipped at its bargain $6,495 price tag. It came with the most powerful engine in its class, the largest wheels and tires, stripes, trim rings, and more. It was the lowest-priced Jeep that year.

million on gross sales of more than $1 billion. It was expected to earn about the same amount for the second quarter and, if extrapolated, might have had its best year ever in 1987, with more than $200 in profits. One executive remarked, "It was as if Renault had decided after nine months that it didn't want to be pregnant." The solid earnings that Jeep was producing would now go into Chrysler's coffers.

By August 1987 the deal was done and Jeep came under the control of yet another new owner. Now it was up to Chrysler to use its greater assets to take Jeep to a new, higher level. It seemed that after so many years of drifting, Jeep had finally found a safe harbor. Yet, the future has a tricky way of not turning out the way some people think it will, and that was going to be the case once again for Jeep. The coming 10 years were destined to be almost as rocky as the previous 10.

in view of what was gained, a virtual money-machine like Jeep, it was a tremendous deal for Chrysler.

What was so odd about all this was that Renault was bailing out just when AMC had finally broken into profitability. In the first quarter of 1987, AMC earned more than $23

One of the most popular vehicles in America in 1987 was the hot-selling Jeep Cherokee Limited, an all-out luxury version of the XJ Cherokee.

CHAPTER 5

The final show vehicle created by American Motors stylists was the Jeep Comanche Thunderchief concept, which appeared in 1987 and predicted a future facelift that unfortunately never went into production.

1988-1998

CHRYSLER IN COMMAND

JEEP THUS BEGAN A NEW CHAPTER in its corporate life. Chrysler's purchase of AMC/Jeep had no effect on the company's 1988 product offerings that were scheduled to debut in fall 1987. By the time the Chrysler deal was completed, the 1988s were ready for introduction, so there was no chance of changing or refining the vehicles beyond what American Motors had already planned. But that was no problem because the product plan laid down by AMC was a good one; the company was solidly profitable and on its way to a greater future. American Motors earned a profit of some $50 million in the first half of 1987 and in all likelihood would have set a new record for profits if it remained an independent. Some AMC executives believed profits would have been as high as $200 million for the year. According to published sources, that number was verified in an informal study Chrysler did a short time later.

The 1988 Jeep line was solid. Comanche added a new model, the two-wheel-drive Eliminator, taking advantage of the potent new six to produce a truly fast sports truck that was as quick as it looked. The Eliminator's standard equipment included the powerful 4.0-liter engine, five-speed transmission, tachometer, alloy wheels, painted grille, and bucket seats. It was the fastest compact pickup on the market and the best-looking too. For those who wanted a sport truck with four-wheel drive, the company now offered the tough Comanche Chief appearance package, similar to the Cherokee Chief.

Sales of the base model Wagoneer had never met expectations, so it was dropped that year, leaving the Limited as the sole Wagoneer XJ offering for 1988. The Grand Wagoneer returned with minor refinements.

THE WRANGLER LINE was the beneficiary of many changes in 1988. Vince Geraci's interior styling team came up with a new package called the Sahara (originally it was supposed to use the Banana Republic brand until that company's requested royalty percentage grew too large). The Wrangler Sahara was available with either coffee or khaki exterior paint and came with khaki-colored wheels and soft top, foglights with protective mesh screens, special body striping, and khaki-colored interior appointments. It was the first desert-themed sport package offered on the small Jeep and it was a beauty. The three other Wrangler models were Base, Sport Décor, and Laredo. Midyear brought a stripped price-leader Wrangler S priced at $8,995 and aimed at the small Japanese 4x4s. It was higher priced than the Suzuki, but so much more robust a vehicle that was really no comparison.

The Cherokee Limited proved so popular that for 1988 a two-door version was added to the model line. Cherokee now offered Base, Pioneer, Chief, Laredo, and Limited models—the most extensive model lineup ever. The powerful 4.0 six was standard equipment on Cherokee and Wagoneer Limited models.

The brawny but ancient J-series pickups returned for one last season. Production was quite low and Chrysler really didn't want them in the lineup anymore so they

were discontinued well before the end of the model year.

To celebrate the 1988 Olympics, the company released a small run of Olympic Edition Wrangler, Comanche, and Cherokee models equipped with six-cylinder engines, alloy wheels, and special stripes.

In September came word that Chrysler would increase Jeep annual production capacity to 403,000 units and was planning to schedule production of 325,000 Jeeps for 1989. The company was adding many Jeep dealers by offering the franchise to existing Chrysler dealers. In the same way that AMC had weeded out weaker Kaiser Jeep dealers, replacing them with stronger AMC stores, Chrysler was now weeding out weak AMC dealers and replacing them with higher-volume Chrysler retailers. The company was also working to increase export sales of Jeep models, and the new production capacity would allow Jeep to put forth a greater effort in that regard. Worldwide demand for Jeeps was rising because the vehicles were now better suited to overseas conditions, such as crowded roads and high fuel costs.

Work was continuing on the small Jeep JJ concept vehicle. Originally it was to be a simple

The public asked for more aggressive-looking trucks and the Thunderchief was the most aggressive-looking of them all. It's a shame Chrysler management didn't okay this model for production.

One idea that was tossed around during the 1980s was introducing a Jeep minivan. Shown here is one designer's idea of what one might look like.

Vince Geraci was the design chief behind the 1988 Jeep Sahara, which initially was to be called the Jeep Banana Republic. The reason that name didn't come to pass was that the two companies couldn't agree on how much Jeep should pay for the right to use the Banana Republic name.

two-door, offered in soft top or removable hardtop versions, but now it seemed that there were too many chefs in the kitchen; executives from various parts of the company were coming in with suggestions for making the new Jeep an even bigger success than was planned, by offering it with a removable soft top, removable hardtop, fixed hardtop, and in a four-door version as well. Each additional suggested model increased the programs costs, which meant the number of vehicles that needed to be sold to turn a profit also went up, and things were beginning to spiral out of control. Meanwhile, other projects within Chrysler were in need of financing, and the program managers were fighting over whose program should get funded.

In calendar year 1988, Jeep dealers retailed 253,454 units in the United States, a new record. With Chrysler behind it, the Jeep brand was poised to set additional new records, both at home and overseas, if only the market didn't become overcrowded and too competitive.

Early in the 1989 model year, Jeep unveiled a concept vehicle named Concept 1. It was a

compact SUV larger than the XJ series and much more modern-looking. It wowed the crowds at the Detroit Auto Show. Little did they suspect they were viewing a thinly disguised version of the all-new Grand Cherokee that would not come to market until 1992 as an early 1993 model.

The 1989 Jeep line was highlighted by another Jeep SUV first: a four-wheel anti-lock brake system, the first that worked on all four wheels and the first able to operate in two- or four-wheel drive. The new brakes were optional

Here we see a series of photos taken in the styling studios of the Jeep JJ, a concept for a new, smaller Jeep vehicle.

on Wagoneer Limited and Cherokee models equipped with the 4.0-liter engine, automatic transmission, and Selec-Trac four-wheel drive. It was the greatest improvement in SUV safety since the introduction of Uniframe construction in 1984, also by Jeep.

For 1989 Cherokee standard equipment was upgraded to include the five-speed transmission, power steering, and extra-capacity fuel tank. A new Cherokee Sport value model appeared, with unique aluminum wheels, 4.0-liter six, and special stripes. Wrangler now offered the Islander package, which replaced the Sport Décor group. Available in Malibu Yellow, Bright Red, Pearl White, and Pacific Blue exterior colors, the Islander included special striping, full carpeting, silver-painted styled steel wheels, a soft top, and outline white letter tires.

The elegant Grand Wagoneer got some interesting updates in 1989, including an overhead console containing interior lights, map lights front and rear, sunglass holder, garage door opener, compass, and outside thermometer. Keyless entry was another

new standard feature. The compact pickup market was fiercely competitive that year, so Comanche was given a series of option package discounts to allow it to offer more equipment for less money.

In a surprising move, Chrysler extended its famous seven-year/70,000-mile powertrain warranty to cover Jeep vehicles, a sign of just how aggressive the four-wheel-drive market had

The Jeep Comanche Pickup was a strong competitor in the compact pickup market and the best-looking of them all.

Although some experts claim there were no 1988 Jeep J-series trucks, there actually were, and this is the only press photo produced for them. The trucks were manufactured for only a short time before Chrysler pulled the plug on them, after 26 years on the market.

become. In a fiercely competitive environment, Jeep retailed 249,170 vehicles in the United States, a good showing in what was a down year for the industry.

For 1990 Jeep added a four-wheel-drive Eliminator model to the Comanche range and brought minor refinements to the Cherokee and Wagoneer. It was going to be a tough year for Jeep because its two domestic competitors, Ford and GM, were introducing four-door versions of their compact sport utilities; previously only Jeep had offered four-door models. With its generous size and decent styling, the Ford Explorer in particular looked to be a tough competitor.

A milestone and sign of the success of the Jeep XJ series came on Thursday, March 22, 1990, when the one-millionth Jeep XJ, a 1990 Cherokee Limited, was produced. It was a four-door, just as 85 percent of all XJ models produced had been. Over the span of a few short years, Jeep XJ had become the most successful line in Jeep history.

Ever since Jeep became a part of Chrysler, there had been a danger that management would try to expand the Dodge truck line by rebadging some of the Jeep vehicles. In a strictly business sense, it was a good way to spread tooling costs that would allow Dodge to develop additional models cheaply. One possibility was to restyle the Wrangler and have it replace the slow-selling Dodge Raider (built by Mitsubishi). Another plan was to create a Dodge compact SUV out of either the Cherokee or an upcoming all-new and larger Jeep coming in the spring of 1992. This was the ZJ, designed by Bob Nixon

and his AMC staff years earlier. It had been temporarily shelved by Chrysler, which wanted to use its product development cash to bring out a pair of redesigned minivans.

The 1988 Wrangler presented the classic Jeep profile, reflecting a heritage that went back 47 years. Jeep enthusiasts complained about the rectangular headlamps, but they continued to buy these great vehicles regardless.

Wrangler is classic Jeep, reflecting a heritage that goes back more than 70 years. Jeep enthusiasts revere them for their iconic looks and legendary performance.

Behind the scenes Jeep stylists and engineers were working on a project to create a vehicle dubbed the JJ, or Junior Jeep. This was to be a small four-cylinder, four-wheel-drive vehicle for both the U.S. and world markets. In this rare drawing, we see the JJ; however, here it is wearing a Renault badge.

The Jeep JJ would have been equipped with a four-cylinder engine, perhaps also a diesel for overseas markets. This clay model shows a handsome four-seater with built-in roll bars and very short overhangs. It's a shame this project didn't reach production.

Dodge dealers liked the idea of finally having a compact SUV to sell, and of course the corporate bean counters at Chrysler were thrilled by the idea of spreading tooling costs over two models rather than one. But naturally the move would greatly dilute the Jeep product image, and it could be the start of a wholesale product-sharing that would eventually reduce Jeep to simply a marketing entity rather than a division that designed and engineered its own unique products. In return for sharing the Jeep products with Dodge, Jeep and Eagle dealers were supposed to get a short-wheelbase four-wheel-drive version of the Chrysler minivan to sell under the Eagle brand. In 1990, the topic of product-sharing was discussed in countless meetings at Chrysler, but no firm decisions had been made, other than tooling for the Eagle van had been ordered. However, it was certain that if Jeep dealers got an Eagle minivan from Dodge, then Dodge dealers would in return get a Dodge-branded Jeep product.

The new competition from Ford and GM had a telling effect on Jeep U.S. retail sales in 1990; they dropped to 196,893 for the year. The company had no new products coming out for 1991, so it was expected that year would be a tough one as well. But help was on the way. The new ZJ was certain to put a spark into 1992 sales. Until then, Jeep dealers had to do the best they could with what they had.

There was cause to celebrate in 1991. It was the 50th anniversary of the first Willys Jeeps going into production. Oddly enough, though, Jeep didn't have much of anything that was really new to show people during this milestone year. The Wrangler line got a sharp new Renegade model powered by a new 180-horsepower 4.0 High Output Six, finally jettisoning the old 258 carbureted six. The Renegade, available in black, white, or red, had color-keyed wheel flares, integrated bodyside steps, aluminum wheels and all-terrain tires, a red interior, and even an optional red hardtop. There was a new sound bar option and new standard multipoint fuel injection for the base four-cylinder engine.

The Wagoneer Limited was dropped that year. Its sales had continued to fall, so it was time to trim it from the line. It was replaced by a new Cherokee Briarwood loaded with goodies such as leather upholstery, teak woodgrain bodyside accents, and air conditioning. The XJ 4.0 six now pumped out 190 horsepower.

Jeep sales tumbled a bit more in 1991, dropping to 177,775 in an extremely competitive market; but help was on the way. In November 1991 workers at an all-new Jeep plant began assembling preproduction models of the all-new 1993 Jeep ZJ. It was revealed then that the new Jeep would be called the Grand Cherokee, and rather than replace the Cherokee, it would be an addition to the lineup. It was the last all-new vehicle from American Motors to reach production.

The elegant Grand Wagoneer was dropped from the line for the 1992 model year. It had been in production since the fall of 1962, making it one of the longest-running vehicles in history, and had been wildly successful, but now, with an all-new Grand Cherokee coming out, Jeep management decided to pull the plug on Grand Wagoneer.

The Cherokee, Wrangler, and Comanche got minor refinements because the focus was going to be on the all-new Grand Cherokee. There was, however, one new Cherokee model for 1992. In an effort to boost volume, Jeep began offering a police version of the carryover Cherokee.

The 1993 Grand Cherokee made its official debut at the 1992 North American International Auto Show in Detroit. It made a stunning entrance, driving up the front steps of Cobo Hall and smashing through the plate glass front doors, spraying glass everywhere. Journalists in attendance went wild over the display of self-confidence and pluck shown by Chrysler.

Jeep called Grand Cherokee a new standard-bearer, because it was another big leap forward for sport utility vehicles. With gorgeous styling by Bob Nixon and his team of Jeep designers, it was the first to offer a standard driver's-side

Another possible Jeep Wrangler model was something called the "Ivory Coast." Although photos of it have not yet surfaced, we do have a picture of the decal that would have adorned its sides.

This has always been the place where the trail ends and the Jeep legend begins.

From the beginning, there have been those special people who've chosen to pursue a path less traveled than the rest. Through a world untamed and unyielding. At times, unforgiving. In search of what can only be found at the furthest outpost of civilization. Where nature begins to reveal her true wonder and magnificence.

We used to call such people *pioneers*.

Today, as it has for nearly five decades, Jeep understands this personal urge to go where the roads do not. For despite others' claims of toughness, no other automotive name evokes a truer, clearer image of places wild and uncharted. For no other family of vehicles was created exclusively to serve and, if you will, to honor that spirit of adventure.

And the freedom to pursue it.

Like most sure-footed creatures adept in wild environs, Jeep has evolved

airbag; it also had the most powerful engine in its class, standard four-wheel antilock brakes, Unibody construction, three four-wheel-drive systems, and a new multi-link Quadra Coil suspension with coil springs at all four corners for the best ride in its class.

But Grand Cherokee was more than just a list of features. It was wide, it was roomy, and it was very, very classy. It offered the most shoulder and front hip room in its class. It set new standards in ride and handling. During suspension development, renowned racecar driver Emerson Fittipaldi served as a consultant to Chrysler, and his efforts showed up in the handling characteristics of the Grand Cherokee. It was clearly the class standout, the best of the best. As one magazine said, "The Ford Explorer, in one fell swoop, has become yesterday's news." It was named "4x4 of the Year" by *Petersen's 4Wheel & Off-Road* magazine, just one of many awards it would win as accolades poured in.

Three models were offered: Base, Laredo, and Limited. Base models lacked the lower bodyside cladding that the other models had, and the interior trim was more basic. Not many were sold, as the public overwhelmingly chose the up-market models. Initially only the 4.0 six and four-speed automatic transmission were offered, but before long a five-speed manual became available.

Command-Trac shift-on-the-fly part-time four-wheel drive was standard on Base and Laredo models, and Selec-Trac was optional. Limited models got the extraordinary Quadra-Trac full-time system, which was also available at extra cost on Base and Laredo.

The new Jeeps were built in an all-new factory on Jefferson Avenue in downtown Detroit, a plant that was the most advanced automobile manufacturing facility in North America and possibly the world. It introduced a new level of quality to the SUV market.

As the all-new Grand Cherokee was readied for introduction, Chrysler management worried that the Jeep dealer network would not be able to sell all the vehicles that the new factory could build. They asked Bob Nixon to have his team come up with a Dodge version of the Grand Cherokee, just in case. This never-before-seen photo shows what it would have looked like.

Work continued for a while on the JJ project. Here we see the original concept as it was envisioned: a simple soft-top two-door SUV with an integral roll bar. A plastic hardtop would have been optional.

Well-meaning people decided to expand the JJ program to include the four-door wagon seen here. While it's an exceptionally attractive vehicle, it complicated things because a four-door requires a completely different body from the two-door, at least from the windshield back. This greatly increased the program's costs, eventually dooming the whole program when management balked at the growing expense.

After some months had passed, a 5.2-liter 220-horsepower V-8 engine became available on Grand Cherokee. In a cheeky print ad Jeep proudly announced, "The good news is Grand Cherokee is now available with a V-8 engine. There is no bad news." A new Grand Wagoneer also debuted for 1993, but it was essentially a fully loaded Grand Cherokee with a standard V-8 and woodgrain side trim and did not prove popular.

The Grand Cherokee, on the other hand, was exactly what the market wanted and its sales took off right from the start. For calendar year 1992, which included 1993 Grand Cherokee sales since its release on April 19, 1992, dealers retailed a total of 268,724 Jeep vehicles in the United States. Nearly 87,000 of those were the new Grand Cherokee.

The rest of the 1993 Jeep line debuted at the normal time, i.e., the fall of 1992. As expected, the Cherokee line was reconfigured to bring it into a lower price range, making it an ideal vehicle to steal sales from Explorer and Blazer, as well as compete with the Japanese SUV's on price as well as features. The Cherokee line was now comprised of Base, Sport, and Country models, with prices starting as low as $12,622 for a two-door two-wheel-drive model.

The Grand Cherokee line added a new two-wheel-drive version for people who didn't think they needed four-wheel drive. The Jeep Comanche, whose sales had been declining for several years, was dropped from the line, and surely that was a mistake on the part of management. The truck market is important to be in, and Jeep management should have tried to revive sales rather than throw in the towel. Perhaps a larger Comanche based on the Grand Cherokee would have sold better. Product planners had considered it but decided not to go ahead with one.

Two years earlier, Jeep dealers had been told by Chrysler management that if they were unable to sell out the full production run of Grand Cherokees, then Dodge dealers would be given a version to sell under the Dodge brand as soon as 1994. It was a tall order, but the Jeep retail network knocked the ball out of the stadium in 1993, with retail sales of Grand Cherokee coming to more than 217,000.

A total of 408,323 Jeep vehicles were sold in the United States that year, a huge hike and another new record. It was an amazing performance.

The 1994 Jeep range saw many improvements. The Wrangler got an easy-operating soft top with full doors, optional new "Add-a-Trunk" storage, an improved torque converter for the automatic transmission and six-cylinder powertrain, and some new colors. Jeep Cherokee also got the new torque converter, along with increased roof crush resistance and side intrusion door beams for greater safety, plus a right-hand-drive Rural Postal Carrier option group, putting Jeep back in the letter-carrier market.

For 1994, Grand Cherokee got upgraded Laredo wheels and tires, new side guard door beams, an integrated child seat, upgraded AM-FM/cassette radio upgrade, and an optional power sunroof. The Base model was renamed the SE. The Grand Wagoneer was dropped for lack of sales.

In January 1992, Jeep unveiled the new Grand Cherokee in stunning fashion when it had one driven through the front glass at Cobo Hall in Detroit during the North American International Auto Show. Although it was a trick—reportedly the glass actually was shattered by small explosives just as the Jeep reached it—any journalist who was there will recall that exciting moment to the end of their days. Nothing like it had ever been done before.

By May 1994, Grand Cherokee sales were through the roof. The company had already expanded production by adding a second shift, raising annual Grand Cherokee capacity to 267,000 units. Now it authorized adding a third shift to raise capacity to 315,000 units. With three full shifts, the plant was essentially running round the clock, 24 hours a day.

Meanwhile, Toledo began producing the Dodge Dakota pickup in the Stickney Avenue plant where Wranglers were also built. There was no parts sharing between the two makes; it was strictly a way of getting more Dakotas while using excess Wrangler capacity.

Jeep enjoyed another good year in 1994 with sales reaching 436,445 units in the United States,

yet another new record. Retails sales of nearly 75,000 Wranglers was also a new record.

By 1995, it was time to add some more spice to Grand Cherokee to keep it fresh and exciting. A new top-line Orvis Edition, named for the famed sporting goods retailer, debuted as a competitor to Ford's popular Eddie Bauer Explorer. The Jeep Orvis included Up-Country suspension, Quadra-Trac four-wheel drive, four-wheel disc brakes, power front seats, dark green and champagne leather interior trim, and more. The exterior was Brilliant Moss Green with Road Red and Maize accents.

Other Grand Cherokee features included a beefed up V-8, standard four-wheel disc brakes on all models, standard automatic

transmission on all models, a new flip-up tailgate window, mini-overhead console with compass, temperature gauge, trip computer and map lights, and asymmetrical off-road tires. The Limited model could now be had in a two-wheel-drive model but only with the 4.0 six.

The 1995 Cherokee got a new standard driver's-side airbag and new reclining front seats based on the Grand Cherokee design. Dual horns were finally made standard equipment. Cherokee offered the SE and Sport models in two- or four-door versions and the upscale

Country as a four-door only. All could be had in two- or four-wheel-drive variations.

For 1995, the Wrangler Renegade was dropped, leaving just the S, SE, and Sahara models. The four-cylinder Wrangler S now offered a new optional appearance package called the Rio Grande, which included Pueblo cloth seats with recliners, full-face styled steel wheels, Bright Mango exterior paint, and Rio Grande decals. SE models could be ordered with a new Sport Group that included bodyside graphics and body-color side steps. In 1995, Jeep sales slipped a bit to 426,628.

Jeep's 1996 model year was one of the strangest in its history because there was no Wrangler offered. Jeep engineers and stylists were in the process of completely redesigning the smallest Jeep with plans to introduce it as early as possible. Management decided to skip the 1996 model year and bring out the new Wrangler in spring 1996 as a very early 1997 model. To ensure that Jeep dealers didn't run out of Wranglers in the meantime, the factory scheduled extra production of 1995 Wranglers to tide them over until the all-new 1997 Wrangler debuted in March.

The 1996 Cherokee was given a heavy-duty battery and alternator as standard equipment, along with an automatic transmission and brake pedal interlock and standard intermittent wipers. There were also new colors available.

The 4.0-liter six was given a new high-tech aluminum piston design, stiffer block, revised camshaft profile, returnless fuel system, and new engine controller, all aimed at greater smoothness, quiet, and durability with improved response at lower rpm.

The 1996 Grand Cherokee was significantly refined and improved. There was a classy all-new Euro-style interior, a new wide-ratio automatic transmission with the V-8 engine,

Reconfigured as a value-priced sport wagon, the 1993 Cherokee continued to sell extremely well. After nine years on the market, it was still the most attractive small SUV you could buy. And it was a genuine Jeep.

With four-wheel drive, a powerful 4.0-liter six under the hood, and excellent handling, the 1994 Cherokee was ideal for police work.

an upgraded front suspension, along with a new grille, front fascia, body cladding, and nameplates. That year only two models were offered, Laredo and Limited, because the slow-selling SE was dropped.

March 1996 brought the new '97 Wrangler, which was another big step forward for Jeep. It was an all-new vehicle yet remained true to the authentic Jeep character. Jeep platform manager Craig Winn explained that the goal was "to make an acceptable road vehicle and an exceptional off-road vehicle." While Wrangler retained its traditional rugged body-on-frame construction, the ladder frame was strengthened, and the suspension was now Jeep Quadra-Coil with coil springs at all four wheels that provided an additional 7 inches of articulation compared to the old leaf-spring

design. Wrangler boasted the best off-highway capability of any stock production vehicle.

Wrangler's interior was all-new and quite an advancement. For the first time, Wrangler offered dual air bags and an integrated heating, ventilating, and air conditioning (HVAC) system. Company designers came up with a neat instrument panel that included a center stack housing the HVAC controls, radio, ashtray, and accessory switches, making it easier to create right- and left-hand drive configurations. All-new seats provided an extra 1.6 inches of travel up front and, thanks to redesigned wheel housings, 6 inches more rear seat width. The Wrangler now had a proper glove box.

But the biggest change made was to its appearance. In a bow to customer complaints, Jeep finally replaced the bent grille and square

A Tradition
Runs Through It.

headlights of the old Wrangler with a modern yet traditional Jeep grille with rounded headlights. Across America Jeep diehards cheered.

On August 27, 1996, President Bill Clinton was on hand in Toledo to help celebrate production of the two-millionth Jeep Cherokee. Bob Nixon's baby was still going strong and enjoying amazing popularity. For the 1996 calendar year, sales of all Jeeps climbed sharply and a total of 509,183 Jeep vehicles were retailed in the United States.

The rest of the 1997 Jeep vehicles debuted in the fall of 1996, and there was another big surprise: The Cherokee XJ was given a $215 million dollar freshening. Much of the change could be seen inside the vehicle. A completely new interior featured a new instrument panel that incorporated a passenger-side airbag and was configured with a center stack to make it easier to create left- and right-hand-drive versions. The HVAC was upgraded with improved air ducting to the front and rear, along with less noise. A new

The Jeep Grand Cherokee Orvis Edition for 1995 packed a lot of sport and luxury into one vehicle with Up-Country suspension, Quadra-Trac four-wheel drive, four-wheel disc brakes, power front seats, leather interior trim, and more. The exterior was Brilliant Moss Green with Roan Red and Maize accents.

As fancy as it was, the Grand Cherokee Orvis could handle the rough stuff with ease.

Here we see the hot new Grand Cherokee 5.9 Limited for 1998 along with a Cherokee Laredo. Note the differences in grille textures and bumpers.

The new-for-1998 Grand Cherokee 5.9 Limited in Deep Slate.

Grand Cherokee Laredo in Flame Red.

| Flame Red (Laredo, Limited) | Dark Rosewood Pearl Coat (Laredo, Limited) | Deep Amethyst Pearl Coat (Laredo, TSi, Limited) | Bright Platinum (Laredo, Limited, TSi, 5.9 Limited) | Deep Slate Pearl Coat (Laredo, Limited, 5.9 Limited) |

21

between-the-seats console included air vents to duct heating and cooling air to the rear seat area. Wingback-style seats from the Grand Cherokee were now standard on Sport models and optional on SE. New door panels and an overhead console with trip computer were other new interior features. The Cherokee was also redesigned for easier servicing.

Exterior changes on the Cherokee included new plastic end caps on bumpers. The rear lift gate, formerly plastic, was now a stamped-steel unit with better fit and easier opening and closing. There were new bodyside moldings on Sport and Country models and a new grille and headlight bezels on all models. The front door quarter glass was eliminated to reduce wind noise, and to improve fit and finish, all exterior body dies were new or reconditioned.

All the detail changes added up to a significantly better Cherokee, a fact borne out when it was named 1997 Four-Wheeler of the Year, an absolutely amazing feat for a design that was now 14 years on the market.

Midyear brought a sporty addition to the Jeep lineup: the Grand Cherokee TSi. It came with a body-color grille, special Highland Grain perforated leather-trim seats with Highland Grain vinyl door trim, and big 16x7 five-spoke cast-aluminum wheels with P225/70R16 Goodyear Wrangler HP outline white letter tires.

At the end of September 1997, Chrysler announced that it was killing off Jeep's companion automobile brand Eagle at the end of September 1998. The loss of the Eagle's extra sales meant that many Jeep dealers would have to find other passenger car franchises to sell, and many would choose Chrysler-Plymouth.

Sales fell a bit for 1997, with 472,872 Jeeps retailed in the United States.

After all the new product news the previous year, the 1998 Jeep line was bound to be mostly carryover and it was, but with many significant improvements. To begin, there was a sharp new model in the Grand Cherokee line, the incredible 5.9 Limited, which featured a 5.9-liter V-8 pumping out 245 horsepower. The big engine made the Grand Cherokee the fastest-accelerating sport utility on the market, capable of 0 to 60 in 7.3 seconds—faster than some European performance cars. It was also the most powerful, fastest, and most luxurious Grand Cherokee to date. Interior features included premium leather seating, a sunroof, a 180-watt stereo with 10 speakers, and a 60–40 rear seat with a fold-down armrest. The

The popularity of customizing Jeep vehicles with factory-approved Mopar accessories was on the rise. Here we see a range of 1998 Jeeps with accessory bumpers, lights, and other equipment.

One of the most exciting concept vehicles ever to spring forth from Jeep stylists was this Jeepster, which revived a classic name on a modern, two-passenger sports machine.

5.9 Limited was priced at $38,700, or $4,385 more than the Grand Cherokee Limited. *Petersen's 4Wheel & Off-Road* magazine named it the "4X4 of the Year." The rest of the Grand Cherokee line—the Laredo, TSi, and Limited—was given minor refinements. The Orvis model was dropped.

The regular Cherokee line had two new models, the Classic and Limited. The Classic was positioned between the Sport model and top-line Limited. It featured monotone exterior paint for a classy look, automatic transmission with 4.0-liter six, power mirrors, roof rack, cast-aluminum wheels, and a leather-wrapped steering wheel. Cherokee Limited replaced the Country model at the top of the line and came with luxury alloy wheels, Selec-Trac four-wheel drive, bodyside paint stripes, rear defroster, air conditioning, leather-trimmed seats, six-way power driver's seat, and much more. It showed clearly that people were interested in more luxury in their Jeep vehicles, not less.

Sales fell a bit in 1998, with some 459,294 Jeeps retailed in the United States. But overseas sales were hot. Jeep sold nearly 31,000 vehicles in Europe alone that year.

But something worse happened to Jeep during 1998 than simply a minor drop-off in sales: Robert Eaton, the Chrysler chairman who replaced Lee Iacocca, negotiated a merger of his company with German automaker Daimler-Benz, maker of Mercedes-Benz automobiles. It was called a "merger of equals" because that was what Daimler-Benz boss Jurgen E. Schrempp told Eaton it would be, at least to his face. But Schrempp had no plans to share power with Eaton or any American. His real motive was to take over one of the most successful automakers in the world and use it as part of his bid to make Daimler the largest car company in the world. Sadly for Jeep, he also had no idea of spending too much money on product development for the great American SUV. In fact, for the next few years Jeep would starve for product funds. Luckily, the company had already scheduled a new product for 1999. It was going to be another hit for Jeep, its last for a while unfortunately.

CHAPTER 6

Despite its fame as one of the most luxurious sports utility vehicles in the world,
Grand Cherokee has always maintained outstanding capability in all driving situations.

1999–2007

THE DAIMLERCHRYSLER FIASCO

THE JEEP LINE FOR 1999, though modest in numbers, was extremely impressive. Cherokee offered four models: SE, Sport, Classic, and Limited. The popular Cherokee Sport got a freshened appearance with the front grille, head lamp bezels, front and rear bumpers, and license plate brow all painted body color. Cherokee Limited now offered heated seats with six-way power adjustment, and all Cherokees benefited from new one-piece weather stripping that reduced noise. Two new colors debuted: Forest Green and Desert Sand.

Jeep Wrangler got the same two colors, along with a new Intense Blue and Medium Fern. Wrangler hardtops and soft tops were available in a new color, Dark Tan. There were some minor mechanical improvements as well. Inside Wrangler were new HVAC controls and Camel/Dark Green seat trim on Sahara. The air conditioner compressor was redesigned for improved performance.

But the big news for 1999 was, of course, the unveiling of the all-new Grand Cherokee. And for once, all-new really meant it—only 127 parts were carryover from the previous Grand Cherokee, and those were mainly screws and fasteners. To illustrate that point, Chairman Bob Eaton held up a small bag filled with the carryover parts to show reporters. It was very impressive.

The 1999 Grand Cherokee was designed to increase the distance between itself and any second-ranked vehicles by offering more luxury, off-road capability, and style than any other vehicle in its class. It surpassed even those lofty goals.

Jeep had begun its slow, careful rollout of its newest Grand Cherokee in January 1998 at the Detroit Auto Show, when they put its new powertrain and four-wheel-drive system on display. Grand Cherokee would introduce an improved 4.0-liter six along with two new engines: an all-new and lighter 4.7-liter V-8 and a new 3.1-liter five-cylinder diesel for international markets. The redesigned 4.0 engine produced 195 horsepower and was both smoother and quieter. The 235-horsepower 4.7 V-8 replaced the outgoing 5.2 V-8 and provided more power and greater durability, along with faster acceleration and better fuel economy. The five-cylinder diesel was a muscular unit produced by VM Motori of Italy, a supplier that would figure prominently in Jeep's future. There was also an all-new electronically controlled automatic transmission with adaptive shifting that could "learn" the owner's driving style and adjust shifts accordingly. The new vehicle also got an entirely new, segment-leading on-demand four-wheel-drive system called Quadra-Drive. This

revolutionary system combined the new Quadra-Trac II patented transfer case with Vari-Lok progressive axles that used speed-sensing gerotor couplings to transfer full torque front to rear and also side to side, seamlessly and automatically. With Quadra-Drive, even if only one wheel had traction, the vehicle could move. It was another outstanding Jeep innovation in four-wheel drive and was unmatched in the industry.

A new suspension system and steering gear provided a quieter, smoother ride and superb off-road performance while the all-new brake system

Top: The regular Cherokee for 1999 offered four models: SE, Sport, Classic, and Limited. The popularity of this iconic Jeep continued and worldwide sales were excellent.

Bottom: For the 2000 model year, the Mopar Navigation System (GPS) became available on Grand Cherokee.

the equal to many high-priced European sports sedans in looks and quality. Taken altogether, the Grand Cherokee was a stunning achievement. Once again, Jeep had come up with the undisputed leader in four-wheel-drive vehicles. Grand Cherokee was, said Jeep, "The Most Capable Sport Utility Ever." *Peterson's 4Wheel & Off-Road* magazine named Grand Cherokee its "4X4 of the Year"—again.

Jeep production soared in 1999, rising to 635,033 units built in the United States, plus a substantial number built at plants in Venezuela, Austria, Argentina, and Thailand. Retail sales in the United States grew to 554,466 Jeeps, just over 300,000 of which were the new Grand Cherokee, putting it on the list of top 10 best-selling vehicles in the United States that year. Even the old Cherokee did well, selling a surprising 165,000 units in the U.S. market. Jeep sales outside the United States totaled 121,028 units, bringing the worldwide total to 675,494 units, a new record. Bob Eaton claimed that over 430,000 Grand Cherokees were built worldwide,

offered best-in-class braking. Big standard 16-inch wheels and tires were another new feature.

Style-wise, the Jeep designers did an exceptional job. Grand Cherokee maintained a strong family resemblance to the previous model yet was longer and featured smoother, more fluid lines. It had a well-defined high-end appearance, with the look and feel of a luxury four-wheel-drive wagon. The interior was completely new as well and was

JEEP CHEROKEE 2001

JEEP 60TH
ANNIVERSARY EDITIONS

ANNIVERSARY EDITION
60 YEARS

Vehicles shown in Silverstone Metallic.
Also available in Black.

The 2001 Jeep 60th Anniversary models. Although total Jeep sales were down this year, they still topped the half a million mark worldwide. There were rumors that Daimler-Benz would sell its Chrysler holdings to cut its losses.

with the balance being sold in foreign markets. Demand in Europe was particularly strong. Eaton also said the company needed still more Grand Cherokees to meet increasing demand.

The following year, 2000, marked another turning point for the Jeep brand. DaimlerChrysler revealed a new long-range program to integrate Jeep retail franchises with Chrysler-brand dealers. The Plymouth brand was being phased out—a move that made little sense—so Chrysler dealers needed to add another line in order to generate enough volume to earn a decent profit. And since the Eagle passenger car was also gone, Jeep dealers needed to add a car line. In that regard, the merging together of two dealer networks made good business sense. But the actual process was going to be tedious and gut-wrenching, since many longtime dealers would be forced to sell or give up their franchises.

After such an extended run of new product announcements, there were only detail changes in the 2000 Jeep line, but some of them were significant. The Mopar Navigation System—what we call GPS today—became available on Grand Cherokee. Cherokee Limited got a bright new grille and aluminum wheels, along with the improved 4.0 six. And Wrangler Sahara now came standard with 6x7 Ultra Star cast-aluminum wheels.

Grand Cherokee had some teething problems with its new progressive axles; there were some complaints of roughness in early units, but the motor press was clearly impressed by their capability. The enthusiast magazine *AutoWeek* wrote, "We were unable to find a situation that would confuse Grand Cherokee's Quadra-Drive four-wheel-drive system—on-road or off. . . . The driver doesn't need to adjust switches or knobs; the system just does what

An interesting new Wrangler model for 2002 was this Apex, which offered exclusive Bright Silver Metallic paint, unique graphics, Cognac Ultrahide seats, and chrome full-faced wheels.

2002 Jeep Wrangler
Apex

apex (a'peks') n. the highest point

it's supposed to do. . . ." It was indeed the most advanced four-wheel-drive system in the world.

However good its systems were, it proved to be a rough year for Jeep. Retail sales in the United States fell to 495,000 units, and worldwide unit sales fell to 604,162. Jeep's parent company was in trouble—profits at Chrysler Group fell 90 percent for the year, and the company actually lost more than $1.5 billion in the second half. The problem was that ever since the merger, the U.S. and German executives had been unable to get along or to agree on very much, and the old Chrysler "Can Do" spirit was being stifled by some rather stiff-necked German managers. Product development was stalled, and the German masters didn't seem to understand the American automotive mass market, where rebates and deals were often used to move the merchandise. They had previously sold only in the upper class

market where such tactics were seldom utilized, and they didn't think it necessary to cut prices to compete in the mid- and lower range of the market—a belief that was quickly proved wrong. Daimler-Benz Chairman Jürgen Schrempp was extremely unhappy with Chrysler, and in November 2000 he forced out Chrysler boss Jim Holden, an earnest and capable leader, replacing him with his own man, the flamboyant and likeable Dieter Zetsche. The Germans were now in full command in the United States.

For 2001, there again was very little new in the Jeep product line, and some journalists wondered if Jeep was losing its edge, or if the German owners were simply withholding product development funds in an effort to boost short-range profits. After all, the Jeep lineup consisted of just three series—Cherokee, Grand Cherokee, and Wrangler. Several

Here's a 2002
Jeep Wrangler, this
one a value-packed
"X" model.

2002 Jeep WRANGLER

THE **LEGEND** LIVES IN WRANGLER.

Experience the ultimate "wind-in-your-hair" freedom in America's off-road fun machine, Jeep Wrangler. Spice up your wardrobe with the new Wrangler X, a rugged and affordable 4x4 that allows you to reach new heights in style. X features a standard 4.0L Power Tech I-6 engine, five-speed manual transmission and Goodyear Wrangler all-terrain tires on 15x7-inch Full-Face wheels. Create your own fun, freedom and adventure in the 2002 Jeep Wrangler.

Wrangler X

Sport (right) and Sahara (middle) join X and SE in the Wrangler lineup. (Far right) Wrangler X cloth interior shown in Agate.

Properly secure all cargo.

competitors offered a much broader ranges of vehicles, including large and small pickups and small SUVs, such as the Toyota Rav-4 and Honda CRV. Jeep had nothing in those categories.

In the 2001 Cherokee line, a new Steel Blue color that replaced Desert Sand was the only new feature worth mentioning, plus the elimination of the four-cylinder engine—the 4.0 six was now standard on all models. Wrangler got a beefier fuel tank skid plate, anti-lock brakes, 100,000-mile engine coolant, quick-removal side steps, and three new exterior colors.

Grand Cherokee received more new features than the other two Jeeps combined. There was an interesting five-speed automatic transmission with two overdrive gears for improved fuel economy and reduced engine noise at highway speeds. There were Euro-style

gathered leather seats on the Limited. There was also a new Laredo Appearance Package available with seven exterior colors. It featured molded-in low-gloss color fascias and cladding in four accent colors, big Michelin P235/65R17 tires on seven-spoke aluminum wheels, leather seating, foglights, and a Light Quartz bodyside stripe. The 4.7 V-8 offered an industry-first hydraulically driven engine fan for reduced noise.

In January 2001, Jeep unveiled a new concept vehicle called the Jeep Willys. It was sort of a Wrangler for the future and featured a composite plastic body, full roll cage, exaggerated wheels and tires, and a handsome new grille. Power came from a supercharged 1.6-liter four-cylinder engine. It proved very popular with the public.

June 2001 brought the end of Jeep Cherokee production in the United States, though it

There was a new Jeep for 2002, the Liberty, which replaced the Cherokee in the U.S. lineup. Liberty was a much more modern vehicle but somehow didn't gain quite the level of love and respect as the Cherokee.

would continue overseas for a while longer. Over 2.7 million Cherokee XJ's had been built since American Motors started production of the 1984 model. Its replacement, a small SUV called the Liberty, had been rumored for some time, and a few spy shots of it had even been published. Soon the public would get to see the new vehicle in showrooms.

Sales took another drop for 2001, with U.S. retail sales coming in at 455,417 vehicles and international sales dropping to 102,736. There was great unrest among DaimlerChrysler's German stockholders, who now questioned the wisdom of tying up with stumbling, money-losing Chrysler, and there were rumors that Chrysler would be sold. Jürgen Schrempp dismissed the rumors outright, vowing to bring Chrysler back to profitability.

At the 2002 Detroit Auto Show, officially known as the North American International Autos Shows (NAIAS), Jeep unveiled a concept vehicle called the Compass. It was meant to

be a small, entry-level Jeep and had the neat styling of a traditional European Rally car, complete with two-doors, bulging fenders, and a rear-mounted spare. Reaction to it was generally favorable.

The big news for 2002 was, of course, the all-new Jeep Liberty. But this new Jeep received a mixed reaction. People liked its size and its roominess, but more than a few were put off by what they saw as a cartoonish grille. The body lines were meant to evoke the handsome Jeep Dakar, a four-door fixed-roof Wrangler concept vehicle that had wowed audiences at car shows. Although the basic shape was about the same, rather than looking rugged and tough like the Dakar, the new Liberty looked cute—something Jeep enthusiasts weren't used to. Those same enthusiasts bemoaned the loss of the Cherokee name as well. Overseas markets didn't have that problem, because in those areas the Liberty wasn't used—the vehicles wore the well-known Cherokee badge.

Liberty was initially offered in just two models, Sport and Limited, and was built in a completely new Jeep-exclusive factory just north of Toledo called, naturally enough, the Toledo North Assembly Plant (TNAP). New high-tech machinery and processes were brought in. Quality levels were very high for the new vehicle, with improved fit and finish compared even to the outgoing Cherokee. Management boasted that these were the most dimensionally accurate Jeeps ever built.

Liberty was the first Jeep with independent front suspension since the original Wagoneer offered it as an option in the early 1960s. Rack and pinion steering was a first for Jeep vehicles and supplied excellent control and feel. On-road refinement was emphasized, with improvements to ride, handling, and noise, yet Liberty could still handle almost any off-road situation. Before being approved for production, it had been tested successfully on the legendary Rubicon Trail—a difficult trek known for killing lesser vehicles.

The chassis was an advanced Uniframe structure that was the stiffest in Jeep history, with coil springs at all four corners to provide excellent ride and articulation. Front and rear stabilizer bars were also included, and they were mounted high so as to not get hung-up off-road.

The standard engine on the Sport was a 2.4-liter four-cylinder engine producing 150 horsepower, which might have been enough for the outgoing Cherokee, but at 3,700 pounds, the Liberty weighed about 400 pounds more than Cherokee, so performance suffered. Most buyers opted for the new 210-horsepower Chrysler 3.7-liter V-6 engine, the first V-6 in a Jeep since 1971. Sport models offered a standard five-speed manual. Limited's came with the automatic as standard equipment.

Liberty could be had in either two- or four-wheel-drive models in a single four-door body style. Command-Trac four-wheel drive was standard, with the premium Selec-Trac system available at extra cost.

At least one valid complaint could be made about the Liberty. Unlike the Cherokee, Grand Cherokee, or the original Wagoneer, Liberty didn't introduce any new innovations to the market, and its styling, while pleasant enough, didn't set any standards either.

Mid-year brought a third Liberty model, the Renegade, which reintroduced a beloved Jeep model name. Liberty Renegade came with an eye-catching silver front fascia accent, extra-wide body-color wheel flares with bright chrome fasteners, Renegade badges, and a standard 3.7-liter V-6 engine.

The Wrangler line debuted an exciting new X model, a name that recalled the sporty and fun Gremlin X of the early 1970s. Wrangler X was a sport/value model that took a base SE and added the 4.0-liter six with five-speed transmission, Nomad cloth front and rear seat trim, styled wheels, and an AM/FM/cassette stereo. The costlier Wrangler Sport was upgraded with standard foglights, tow hooks, and full hard doors. Coming mid-season was the Wrangler Apex, a limited-edition value model. The Apex boasted a Bright Silver metallic exterior, unique Apex strobe graphic, high-bolstered earth-tone Ultrahide seating, full-face chrome wheels, an AM/FM/CD seven-speaker stereo, and a full center console, all for just $20,385. Wrangler Sahara now came with the 30-inch tire and wheel group.

There was a lot that was new on Grand Cherokee for 2002. The lineup included a new Laredo Sport value model with standard foglights, heated leather seats, dual heated mirrors, and AM/FM/CD player. There was also a very luxurious new top-of-the-line model, the Grand Cherokee Overland, which offered as standard equipment special fascia treatments,

The 2003 model year saw the unveiling of a new Jeep vehicle destined to become another icon, the awesome Wrangler Rubicon, the most capable Jeep ever. With specially designed axles and transfer case, the Rubicon answered the need for buyers interested in extreme off-roading.

protective rock rails, 17-inch Hammerhead aluminum wheels, two-tone leather and suede interior, real Redwood Burl interior wood trim, and a long list of standard luxury features.

A new high-output (HO) version of the 4.7-liter V-8 debuted, good for 265 horsepower and an excellent 325 lb-ft of torque. It was standard on the Overland and optional on the others; the 4.0-liter six remained standard equipment on other Grand Cherokees, and the carryover 235-horsepower version of the V-8 was also available. There were new luxury items: a power adjustable pedal system and rain-sensitive windshield wipers, along with new safety in the form of side-curtain airbags and a tire-pressure monitoring system.

Despite the new Liberty and the Wrangler and Grand Cherokee models, Jeep sales were stagnant for 2002, coming in at 459,796 units in the United States—or about 95,000 units less than 1999. Outside the United States, however, Jeep sales rose to 120,637 units.

The 2003 model year introduced another iconic Jeep vehicle—the incredible Wrangler Rubicon. Named after the world-famous Class Ten off-road trail (the toughest rating), the new Jeep Rubicon was designed to be the most capable factory-stock off-roader available. As Jeep explained at the unveiling, "The new 2003 Jeep Wrangler Rubicon is engineered to take on the most demanding trails, including those previously reserved for only highly modified vehicles." Craig Love, vice president of the Jeep Product Team said, "The 2003 Jeep Wrangler Rubicon features an off-road performance package as only Jeep can engineer, allowing serious off-road enthusiasts the opportunity to drive over some of the most extreme trails in the country, and then drive it home."

Wrangler Rubicon certainly had the guts to do the job. It featured front and rear Dana model 44 axles and a 4:1 low-range transfer case. Also featured were advanced Tru-Lok locking

differentials that could be driver-actuated when the transfer case was in low range with vehicle speed below 10 miles per hour. A dash-mounted rocker switch allowed the driver to lock the rear axle and toggle the front axle locker switch on and off for improved maneuvering. When engaged, the feature mechanically locked the axle shafts together to drive all four wheels at the same speed—just as the original Quad-Trac Emergency Drive had done in the 1970s. When unlocked, the rear axle offered a torque-sensing limited-slip feature to provide better traction and handling on-road. The Rock-Trac transfer case could slow vehicle speed to give the driver more control and increase the amount of torque available at the wheels. This special fixed-output NV241 Off-Road transfer case was engineered specifically for the Wrangler Rubicon to meet the demanding durability requirements of an intense off-road vehicle. For the same reason, Rubicon also included heavy-duty driveshafts and universal joints. Goodyear Wrangler "Maximum Traction/ Reinforced" 31-inch tall tires featured a beefy tread pattern that wrapped around the sidewall

The 1999 Grand Cherokee was all-new from the tires up, with only 127 minor parts carried over from the previous generation. Boldly styled and packing a great deal of new technology, the Grand Cherokee was once again the best SUV wagon you could buy.

The Israeli Army used locally assembled Jeeps for the armed forces. Here we see an Israeli Jeep patrolling the border.

to help grab ledges along the trail. The new state-of-the-art off-road tires included a three-ply sidewall and advanced silica compound for excellent durability and puncture resistance. Said Love, "This combination of what would typically be aftermarket hardware provides tremendous off-road capability to give our enthusiast owners a rig that is ready for their favorite trails, right out of the box." Rubicon also came with diamond-plate side steps and unique exterior graphics.

Wrangler benefited from a new four-speed automatic transmission option that provided better fuel economy and quieter engine operation. There was also a new standard mill for Wrangler. Offering significantly more horsepower and torque, the Jeep Liberty's 2.4-liter Power Tech I-4 replaced the 2.5-liter I-4 as the standard engine on 2003 Jeep Wrangler SE models. The new engine provided 150 horsepower at 5,200 rpm—a 25-percent increase—and 165 lb.-ft. of torque at 4,000 rpm, an 18-percent increase in torque. The 2.4-liter engine was also quieter, more fuel-efficient, and said to be engineered for longer life and ease of maintenance.

There was also an all-new interior for Jeep Wrangler. New front seats provided an additional 20 millimeters of rearward travel for extra room, while taller seat backs provided a more comfortable ride. There was a lever on the side of the front passenger seat for easy access to the rear.

In addition to new front and rear seats, the 2003 Jeep Wrangler also featured a electrochromic rearview mirror that included map lights, temperature, and compass display. It was standard on Sahara, optional on Sport and Rubicon models. There was also a four-spoke steering wheel and available Dark Slate or Khaki interior trim. Jeep management noted that by this point, Jeep Wrangler was being sold in 100

countries around the world and was available in right- and left-hand-drive versions.

There wasn't much change to Jeep Liberty for 2003. As before, there were three models: Sport, Limited and Renegade. A new overhead console, based on the Grand Cherokee design, included the ability for customers to program the operation of nine convenience and safety items to their own requirements, including which doors would unlock with the remote keyless entry unlock button, what mileage was desired between service intervals, and the amount of time the headlamps remained on after exiting the vehicle. New was an available six-disc in-dash CD player that replaced the remote CD changer seen the previous year. More important, four-wheel disc brakes were now standard.

For 2003, Grand Cherokee received numerous suspension revisions to reduce steering effort, improve ride and handling, and provide improved

For many years in the 1960s and 1970s, Sarao Motors built Jeep-based "Jeepney" taxicabs in the Philippines. In time the Jeepney became a national symbol.

brake feel. Grand Cherokee was given reduced-pressure shocks, new brake calipers for a lighter brake pedal feel, and a revised steering-gear torsion bar. The improvements, said Jeep, created "the smoothest and most responsive Jeep Grand Cherokee ever, without sacrificing any of the vehicle's on-road or off-road capability." There were also new ceiling-mounted side-curtain air bags that provided additional head protection for both front and rear outboard occupants.

But the 2003 Grand Cherokee model year was probably the shortest in Jeep history because by January 2003, a revised and improved 2004 Grand Cherokee debuted. There was a handsome new fascia, grille, and foglights on all Grand Cherokee models, along with two new colors: Midnight Blue and Lava Red. There was a new Special Edition model that included the 4.0-liter

six, four-speed automatic, Quadra-Trac II transfer case, and an AM/FM/10-disc CD player. Interestingly, there was also a new single-speed Quadra-Trac I transfer case for Laredo models, meant for the 85 percent of owners who didn't take their Jeeps off-road; Jeep hadn't offered a single-speed transfer case in years. All Grand Cherokee models were available with two-wheel or four-wheel drive, and factory-installed Navigation Radio was a new option.

Also in January 2003, Jeep introduced a line of special Freedom Edition vehicles at the North American International Auto Show in Detroit. Each was unique. The Grand Cherokee Freedom Edition, which was on the early 2004 model, included the 4.0-liter six, four-speed automatic, high-back cloth seats with the Jeep logo, chrome tow hooks, and Freedom Edition badge. The Liberty Freedom Edition used "bolt-on" flares like the Renegade plus graphite-painted grille, front and rear fascia, and body-color side moldings. Black sidewall P235/65R17 tires were mounted on 17-inch graphite-painted wheels. Wrangler Freedom got P225/75R15 tires on chrome wheels, plus air conditioning, Sentry-Key anti-theft system, Fold-and-Tumble rear seat, and Dark Slate cloth or vinyl seats. In Canada, the Freedom Editions were called Rocky Mountain, and for overseas markets, they were called the Red River Editions.

In February 2003, a Jeep executive let slip that a new Wrangler-based Scrambler pickup was coming in mid-July 2004, and that 20,000 units would be built annually. But he was wrong. A prototype did in fact exist and was being tested, but no Scrambler pickup would appear in 2004—or for a long time after.

Despite the new models, Jeep production fell slightly for 2003, and worldwide retail sales fell to 564,252, about 16,000 less than 2002. At the time, Jeep had full manufacturing facilities (as opposed to simple assembly operations) in the United States, Austria, China, Egypt, Venezuela, and Thailand.

Jeep had gotten a jump on the 2004 model year when it introduced the Grand Cherokee in January 2003. The other 2004 Jeep series were introduced at the normal time, during the fall of that year.

Jeep Liberty for 2004 offered two new colors, Deep Molten Red and Timberline Green. Renegades now offered Rock Rail Protection and black bodyside molding. All Libertys also got a larger, 19.5-gallon fuel tank. New options included a Cargo Organizer and UConnect hands-free cellular capability (Bluetooth) available as a factory-installed option. An AM/FM/CD radio was now standard on all models.

To inject a little more fun in the Wrangler line, two bright new colors were introduced for 2004: Electric Lime Green and Solar Yellow. Tilt steering was standard on all models. Right-hand-drive models were now offered for the U.S. retail market, aimed mainly at Rural Delivery postmen. Later in the model year came a special Jeep Wrangler Willys model, with exclusive military-looking Moss Green paint, a Willys decal on the cowl side, diamond-plate sill guards, body-color wheel flares, AM/FM/CD player, the 4.0 six, foglights, and more.

Then mid-season brought a surprise: a new Wrangler Unlimited model that was 15 inches longer than the standard Wrangler on a 10-inch longer chassis. Offered only as a two-door, the Unlimited was meant to appeal to buyers who needed more interior space; there was now

In 2004 Jeep introduced the "Trail Rated" concept, which in time would allow the company to introduce Jeep vehicles with less off-road capability, serving the new market of buyers who were looking for a smooth-riding on-road four-wheel-drive vehicle.

2 inches more rear leg room and 13 inches more cargo space. The base price was $24,995.

Jeep also introduced the new "Trail-Rated" designation for 2004, to "communicate to consumers the extensive level of off-road requirements that all Jeep vehicles must meet," i.e., a series of tests proving its off-road prowess. But of course the new label could also get people used to the idea that not every Jeep vehicle in the future would by nature be capable of extreme off-roading. They would be able to tell them apart by the badge.

May 2004 brought news that Dodge dealers were going to get a spinoff of the Jeep Liberty. While that was not welcome news to most Jeep dealers, Chrysler assured them that the Dodge product, to be called the Nitro, would have a completely different body. But it did mark a change in product philosophy; previously no other DaimlerChrysler product had shared a chassis with Jeep.

U.S. Jeep sales slid a bit for 2004, to 427,239 vehicles. Overseas sales likewise fell, to 116,202.

Things were looking up for 2005, however. There was a flood of new product news. In the Wrangler line, there was a new Rubicon Unli-mited, marrying the long-wheelbase Wrangler with the Rubicon's extreme-duty mechanicals. This expanded Wrangler's lineup to seven distinct models: SE, X, Sport, Rubicon, Unlimited, Unlimited Rubicon, and Right-Hand Drive.

Jeep Liberty exterior received new fascias, bumpers, grilles, bodyside moldings, and sill moldings. Renegade models got a new front-end appearance, including a flatter hood; a taller, more upright grille; and molded-in accent color fender flares. The interior was freshened with new lighter colors, new front seat contours and fabrics, and a flatter-folding rear seat. Air conditioning was made standard on Sport.

There was also a new four-cylinder diesel Liberty CRD (Common Rail Diesel), which offered the fuel economy of a four-cylinder engine, the performance of a six, and the torque of a V-8—an enormous 295 lb-ft worth. With 160 horsepower, the Liberty CRD was rated at 22 miles per gallon city and 27 miles per gallon highway.

But Jeep's biggest news for 2005 was the arrival of an all-new Grand Cherokee. And again, it really was all new, from bottom to top. Although it was 5.3 inches longer, Jeep stylists

During 2005, Jeep studied the idea of introducing a pickup truck to the line. Several concepts were reviewed, but in the end nothing seemed practical. Jeep should have looked to its past at this 1983 CJ-10 pickup, which was sold in overseas markets, primarily Australia. It used a CJ-7 cab on a J-series chassis.

From the 1950s to the 1960s, a company called Viasa built Jeep vehicles in Spain for the local market. Note the nameplate on the grille of this CJ-3B.

were able to minimize bulk by giving the new Grand Cherokee a more upright, slab-sided look. The beloved 4.0-liter six-cylinder engine, one of the last vestiges of American Motors (the basic engine had been around since the 1964 Rambler) was replaced by a 3.7-liter V-6 good for 210 horsepower, standard on Laredo. Standard on Limited and optional on Laredo was the 4.7-liter V-8. And for the first time ever on a Jeep vehicle, a 5.7-liter Hemi V-8 producing a staggering 325 horsepower was optional on Limited models.

Grand Cherokee's styling was meant to evoke that of the Commander concept, which had won praise in public showings. And it did vaguely resemble it, though unfortunately not enough. Grand Cherokee's styling was pleasant, even elegant. But unlike previous Grand Cherokees, it was not head-turning, nor was it revolutionary.

Three four-wheel-drive systems were offered: Quadra-Trac I with a single-speed transfer case, Quadra-Trac II with a two-speed transfer case, and Quadra-Drive for the ultimate in traction and control. There was also a new suspension for a better ride and, for the first time on a Grand Cherokee, rack and pinion steering to provide outstanding feel and control.

Grand Cherokee was part of a push to get Jeep moving in the right direction, because the truth was Jeep was falling behind. In 1999, Jeep held 19 percent of the SUV market, but by 2003 that had fallen to 9.9 percent, so clearly Jeep was being outpaced by the competition once again.

In January 2005, Jeep showed off a new extended-cab concept pickup called the Gladiator, with Wrangler styling and room for four. It was one of the most talked-about Jeep concepts in years, proof enough that enthusiasts were looking for a truck from Jeep.

In March 2005, Jeep launched three new limited-edition models—Wrangler, Grand Cherokee, and Liberty Rocky Mountain editions—which featured minor trim changes

The four-door Wrangler was a game-changer for Jeep, and it has since become the most popular and profitable model in the Wrangler series.

and badges. Wrangler standard equipment now included a new six-speed manual transmission that replaced the five-speed manual, full-size spare tire on all models, and full-face steel wheels standard on SE, X, and Sport models. Air conditioning was made standard on Sport and Rubicon, along with a seven-speaker stereo system. There was also a new six-disc in-dash CD changer option.

At the New York Auto Show on March 23, 2005, a new Jeep production model was on display. The new Jeep Commander (which had no relationship to the Jeep Commander concept) was a large, seven-passenger SUV with styling that managed to be part Hummer, part Range Rover, and part Cherokee XJ, yet not as good-looking as any of those. It was BIG and expected to bring in a whole new wave of buyers who had previously shunned Jeep because of its lack of a full-size SUV.

The 2005 model year saw a sharp turnaround in Jeeps fortunes, with worldwide retail sales of 608,971.

For 2006, the Jeep Commander went on sale, the first Jeep vehicle ever to offer three rows of seating. Two models were offered: Commander and Commander Limited. Though built on a Grand Cherokee platform, Commander was 2 inches longer and 4 inches taller and looked much more massive than those numbers would indicate. It used the Grand Cherokee drivetrain as well, so the only reason to buy a Commander over a Grand Cherokee was for the extra room and, if one liked a large vehicle, for its imposing size.

After an absence of two decades, Wrangler brought back an old, beloved name in 2006: Golden Eagle. The new Wrangler Golden Eagle Edition featured a Dana 44 heavy-duty rear axle, gold 15-inch Ravine aluminum wheels, 30-inch tires, two-tone premium seats, and Golden Eagle hood, fender, and spare tire decals.

Wrangler Unlimited offered three models: Unlimited Base, Unlimited Premium, and Rubicon Unlimited. The new Premium version of Unlimited came equipped with a chrome grille, body-color fender flares, premium two-tone cloth seats, and silver-painted instrument panel and center stack bezels.

The 2006 model year also saw the return of the Grand Cherokee Overland at the top of the line. Overland was available in both 4x2 and 4x4 models and came standard with the 5.7-liter Hemi V-8, five-speed automatic, and a comprehensive list of standard features.

Also new—and much more exciting—was the Grand Cherokee SRT/8. Powered by a mighty 6.1-liter Hemi V-8, Grand Cherokee SRT8 offered the ultimate in SUV performance. It could do 0–60 miles per hour in less than five seconds, which was quicker than the Porsche Cayenne Turbo or the BMW X5. Its rocket-like acceleration blew away the competition.

Jeep Liberty offered the same four models as before, with the diesel engine now available on Sport and Limited 4x4 models. The 3.7-liter V-6 engine became the standard engine, and the four-cylinder engine was no longer available in the United States.

Jeep had a decent year for 2006, though worldwide sales fell about 13,000 units. The loss was all in the U.S. market; overseas sales rose slightly.

There were a flurry of new product announcements at Jeep for the 2007 model year that included two brand-new vehicles and one completely redesigned vehicle.

There was a new entry-level Jeep this year, something dealers had been asking for. The new Jeep Patriot looked like a conventional four-door SUV—in fact, it looked like a close cousin to the old Cherokee XJ—but it actually was a crossover vehicle, an SUV built on a passenger-car chassis. The reason for designing an SUV that way is that it creates a vehicle with a smoother ride and better fuel economy. In Patriot's case, it was built on the same platform and in the same plant as the front-wheel-drive

Following the Jeep Patriot by a few months was the Compass, a second Jeep based on the Dodge Caliber platform. Compass was aimed at women buyers and featured more car-like styling. It did not offer a Trail-Rated version.

Dodge Caliber compact car. Like Caliber, the base Patriot was a front-driver, but four-wheel-drive versions were the more popular models. Jeep promised that though the basic four-wheel drive Patriot was not "Trail-Rated," it was the most capable four-wheeler in its class. In addition, Patriot could also be ordered in a "Trail-Rated" off-road capable model as well.

Base price for a front-wheel-drive version was $14,958 including shipping, the lowest Jeep price in many years. That price included standard side-curtain air bags, split folding rear seat, Ultra Floor removable vinyl load floor, electronic stability control (ESC), traction control, antilock brake system (ABS), and Electronic Roll Mitigation. Patriot was powered by a 2.4–liter, 170-horsepower four-cylinder engine good for up to 30 miles per gallon, hooked up to a continuously variable transmission (CVT).

Another new Jeep debuting this year was the Compass, built on the same platform as the Patriot/Caliber. Compass was styled much like the Compass concept vehicle that had been shown earlier, except it had four-doors, was less rugged/more feminine-looking, and was meant to attract more women to the Jeep brand. Compass specifications were the same as Patriot's, and it too offered front and four-wheel-drive versions, though Compass didn't offer a Trail-Rated model. Surprisingly, the Patriot and Compass models got off to a fairly slow start, selling only about 40,000 units each during 2008.

Jeep Wrangler had a great year in 2007. It was completely redesigned, with a flat roof, unique door opening line, canted grille, and sloping hood. Three models were offered: Wrangler X, Sahara, and Rubicon. Nearly everything about it was bigger: width was increased by 5.5 inches, length by 2.6 inches, and wheelbase by 2 inches. There were increases in leg, hip, and shoulder room as well. New options included

an innovative three-piece modular hard top that offered several ways to enjoy open air motoring, full-screen navigation radio, power windows, and power door locks. The venerable 4.0-liter straight six was replaced by a new 3.8-liter V-6 good for 202 horsepower. Four-wheel antilock disc brakes were standard across the board. Frame "bending strength" was doubled, and a new electronic-disconnecting sway bar was offered. To introduce it in a memorable way, a Jeep executive once again smashed through the front door of Cobo Center in Detroit, then drove it outside and up to rest atop a fabricated mountain—quite a display of power and capability.

An all-new four-door Wrangler Unlimited also debuted—at last—and it was an immediate hit. Riding a 116-inch wheelbase, it was very large compared to earlier Jeeps and offered plenty of interior room for five people. It was offered in the same three models as the regular Wrangler. Meanwhile the two-door Unlimited was dropped from the U.S. market. The four-door Wrangler proved unbelievably popular. Within weeks, Jeep dealers were reporting shortages, and by March, Wrangler sales were up 63 percent and there was a 45-day wait for ordered vehicles.

Something big happened during the year. In May 2007, the nine-year, $36 billion merger of Chrysler and Daimler-Benz was dissolved. Chrysler was sold for a mere $7.4 billion to Cerberus Capital Management, which took an 80.1-percent stake in the automaker. Cerberus promised to restore Chrysler "to the first ranks of the U.S. and global auto industry." The investment company, which had little to no experience in the automobile business, also acquired responsibility for Chrysler's health and retirement liabilities, its so-called legacy costs, which were substantial. For Daimler-Benz, it was a financial bloodbath.

Jeep developed special models for certain overseas markets, including this Grand Cherokee Laredo Aspen designed for Japan.

"We obviously overestimated the potential of synergies," Dieter Zetsche said at a news conference at the company's headquarters in Stuttgart, Germany. "I don't know if any amount of due diligence could have given us a better estimation in that regard."

For Chrysler workers, there was a sense of relief; they'd never got used to Germans barking orders at them rather than using the American way of trying to gain consensus. And they had felt betrayed when then-Chairman Jürgen Schrempp admitted in an interview that the so-called "merger of equals" was, in fact, a lie. He had never had any thought of sharing power with Bob Eaton or any American. Daimler-Benz had taken over Chrysler by lying and cheating and since then had run it into the ground, so there was cause for the bitter feelings at Chrysler Group. With such a history of deception, the combined company was bound to be a failure. Reporter Bill Jamieson called the merger a fiasco.

But now Jeep and its parent company were owned by people who had scant experience in the auto industry and were investors looking to make a buck. Everyone at Jeep wondered what was next.

火から冬の休日を、おおらかに愉しむ。 特別な魅力を装備した、アスペン登場!

Jeep Grand Cherokee Laredo ASPEN

ジープ・グランドチェロキー ラレード 特別限定車［アスペン］ 全国限定1,000台

CHAPTER 7

Toward the end of 2018, Jeep unveiled its upcoming 2020 Wrangler-based Gladiator pickup
which enthusiasts had been requesting for years. Response to the new truck was extremely good,
and sales were surprisingly strong.

2008-2020

THE ROAD TO THE TOP

THE 2008 MODEL YEAR BROUGHT a completely redesigned, more masculine, and noticeably larger Jeep Liberty. All-new suspension and (optional) Selec-Trac II full-time four-wheel drive debuted, plus a neat Sky-Slider full-open canvas roof option, providing the feel of an open convertible with the safety of a steel roof structure.

Meanwhile, Grand Cherokee received an all-new 4.7-liter V-8 delivering 30 percent more horsepower, 10 percent greater torque, and 5 percent better fuel economy. It featured refreshed interior and exterior design and new amenities, including Sirius Backseat TV and a MyGIG Multimedia Infotainment System with built-in navigation, audio, and entertainment, plus a communication system. Other new additions included high-intensity discharge (HID) headlamps with three times greater light output and auto-leveling that adjusted the headlamps to the vehicle pitch depending on the load and number of passengers. Another important new safety feature was the ParkView back-up camera.

Jeep got some military business with its tough new J8, based on the Wrangler Unlimited, with reinforced frame and axles, plus brakes and suspension engineered for ultra-demanding military use. J8s came with Command-Trac four-wheel drive and a 2.8-liter four-cylinder turbodiesel producing 158 horsepower and 295 lb-ft of torque mated to a beefed-up five-speed automatic. Available as a two-door short-bed pickup or as a four-door multipurpose vehicle, the J8 could be ordered with either right- or left-hand drive and could also be armored. It was well-suited as a command vehicle, troop/cargo carrier, ambulance, or communications vehicle. Production was scheduled for Jeep's joint-venture plant in Cairo, Egypt, in spring 2008.

Jeep boasted seven models for 2008, the most in its 65-year history. "Jeep is the Swiss Army knife of the SUV market," said John Plecha, director of Jeep Marketing and Global Communications. "No other automotive manufacturer in the world has the range of sport-utility vehicles that Jeep has."

U.S. financial markets were in decline, however, and as the economy sank, automotive sales plummeted. In 2008, Jeep worldwide sales slid to just 497,078—a drop of more than 151,000 units. Hard times were coming and Jeep would have a new owner at their close.

The 2009 Patriot and Compass received new interiors, including the instrument panel, door-trim panel, center console, and door armrests. The removable load floor was now carpeted, and illuminated cup holders were new. The pair also benefited from improved engine compartment and floor silencers, plus revised exhaust tuning to quiet driveline noise. Liberty received only minor enhancements, as did Wrangler.

More spartan than modern Jeep vehicles, this vintage CJ-3B still has what it takes for serious off-roading.

A silver Jeep Commander is shown here blasting through the sand. During 2009, Jeep's parent company was forced to file for protection under U.S. bankruptcy laws. In need of financing, the company had been unable to come to agreement with its creditors for an outside-of-bankruptcy restructuring plan.

Grand Cherokee's improvements for 2009 included a tire-pressure monitoring system. There was also a larger 9-inch rear DVD screen and an iPod interface available with the UConnect GPS system. A new 5.7-liter HEMI engine was offered on all models.

But financial markets continued to implode. Sales tanked, and Chrysler was being bled white. With nowhere to borrow needed funds, on April 30, 2009, Chrysler LLC filed for bankruptcy. Cerberus Capital, Chrysler's owner, was unable to find a buyer. General Motors expressed strong interest in merging with Chrysler, but GM itself was two months away from bankruptcy. The courts and the government tried to find a buyer, but only Italian automaker Fiat expressed interest.

On May 31, 2009, the bankruptcy court approved a government restructuring plan and sale of Chrysler's assets. Most of Chrysler was acquired by a new company in which Fiat owned 20 percent; Chrysler's union retirement health care trust owned 55 percent with the balance owned by the U.S. and Canadian governments. Under the deal, bondholders received 29 cents on the dollar; stockholders got nothing. Chrysler's huge legacy costs were slashed, more than 700 small dealers were terminated, and all of Chrysler's so-called "toxic assets" (obsolete or redundant plants) were transferred to an entity known as Old Carco, which was later dissolved. They named the new surviving company Chrysler Group LLC. The federal government financed the $6.6 billion deal.

Despite its minority ownership, Fiat would take charge at Chrysler. The long-term plan was for the Italian firm to acquire a controlling interest, with Fiat chairman Sergio Marchionne wanting to expand Jeep sales in Europe and China, where they were underperforming. He sought to utilize Fiat technology to make Jeep vehicles more fuel efficient to better compete in world markets and to produce all-new, highly fuel efficient Jeep "world" models in underutilized European Fiat plants.

As the economy continued to sicken, Jeep sales for 2009 reached just 337,716 vehicles, Jeep's worst showing since 1992.

For 2010, the company introduced useful improvements to Wrangler and Wrangler Unlimited. The Sunrider soft-top was easier to remove and a fuel saver indicator, fog lamps, and tow hooks became standard on all models. New Satin Silver 18-inch aluminum wheels became standard on Sahara, with Satin Carbon 17-inch aluminum wheels standard on Rubicon.

Mid-year saw the return of the Wrangler Islander after a twenty-year hiatus. The graphics were new and the vehicle now came with Moab 17-inch wheels with big tires, custom interior accents, and special decals. There was also a new limited-edition Wrangler Mountain based on the Sport S.

Once again Jeep Patriot offered three drive configurations: front-wheel, Freedom Drive full-time four-wheel (with lock mode), and Freedom Drive II, an off-road-capable full-time four-wheel drive "Trail Rated" by Jeep. New options included a remote start and automatic climate control on Limited models.

Grand Cherokee had only two new models, Laredo and Limited, which were offered at announcement time. Liberty's standard equipment was upgraded again. Not much was

This vintage vehicle is a mid-1960s Viasa Jeep produced in Spain. Notice how long the body is; this is the long-wheelbase CJ-6 model.

new on Jeep Commander either. The big SUV never met sales expectations, and this was its last year.

But 2010 saw the beginning of a turnaround, with worldwide Jeep sales climbing to 419,516. The economy was rebounding, with buyers beginning to feel more confident.

Things looked even brighter for 2011, which marked Jeep's 70th anniversary. An all-new Grand Cherokee offered a choice of three four-wheel-drive systems, a new Jeep Selec-Terrain system with five terrain settings, plus the new Jeep Quadra-Lift air-suspension system that lowered the Grand Cherokee on the road for better fuel economy and then raised it for off-roading. Also new was a 3.6-liter Pentastar V-6 rated 16 miles per gallon city and 23 miles per gallon highway.

Grand Cherokee boasted more than forty-five safety and security features, including electronic stability control, side-curtain and seat-mounted side air bags, active head restraints, blind-spot monitoring, Rear Cross Path detection system, adaptive cruise control, and forward collision warning, plus an all-weather package for harsh environments.

Also new was the Grand Cherokee Overland Summit, the most luxurious and comprehensively equipped Jeep ever.

A special Grand Cherokee 70th Anniversary Edition debuting in 2010 offered polished 20-inch aluminum wheels with Mineral Gray pockets, Dark Olive leather seats with Chestnut accent stitching, center console in Dark Olive perforated leather with Chestnut stitching, black leather-wrapped steering wheel, Berber floor mats, and a 70th anniversary badge. The special model featured graphite exterior paint and Black Lacewood interior finish.

The company gave Compass new styling up front for 2011 in response to criticism the Compass's front-end styling had received since its debut. Jeep also upgraded its steering and suspension to offer a Trail-Rated version with the new Freedom Drive II Off-Road package. Patriot shared Compass's interior improvements and received minor styling revisions.

The 2011 Jeep Wrangler featured all-new interiors, improved ergonomics, upgraded materials, an all-new body-color hardtop for Sahara, heated power mirrors and seats, plus steering-wheel controls for the radio, cruise control, and hands-free phone. Standard safety equipment now included electronic stability control, hill-start assist, and trailer-sway control. Acoustical materials were added to reduce interior noise.

Wrangler and Unlimited also offered special 70th Anniversary Edition models with unique 18-inch wheels, Dark Olive seats with Chestnut accent stitching, plus satin chrome HVAC rings, front-door pulls, and passenger grab handles. There were also Berber floor mats and Mopar brushed-aluminum sill plates.

Another new Jeep for 2011 was the special-edition Wrangler Mojave. Based on the Sport, Mojave offered a unique desert theme with a body-color hardtop and fender flares, "Mojave" and lizard decals on the hood and rear, plus body side steps. Mojave also included an aggressive Wrangler Rubicon tire and wheel package with mineral gray 17-inch wheels and 32-inch tires.

Inside, the seats were dark saddle leather, with an embossed lizard logo on the front seats. Mopar tread-pattern slush mats and overhead grab handles were included. There was also a new limited-edition Wrangler Call of Duty: Black Ops Edition that year.

For 2011, Jeep added the Liberty Jet premium model with 20-inch polished aluminum wheels, P245/50R20 all-season tires, chrome lower-fascia opening, bodyside moldings, license plate brow, roof rails, mirror caps, blacked-out headlamps, and "Jet" badges. Inside was a nine-speaker premium audio system, a standard security system including supplemental side-curtain air bags and Park Sense park assist, heated front seats, and a leather-wrapped steering wheel with audio controls.

During the third quarter of 2011, Jeep released the new 2012 Grand Cherokee SRT8, the most-powerful, best-performing Jeep ever. Its 6.4-liter HEMI V-8 delivered an estimated 465 horsepower and 465 lb-ft of torque. The big Jeep could do 0–60 mph in 4.8 seconds and mid-13-second quarter-mile times, with a top speed of 155 miles per hour. It was also the best-handling Jeep ever due to an advanced adaptive damping suspension. The new SRT8 could do up to 0.9 g on the skid pad, better than some sports cars.

Jeep's business improved exponentially in 2011 with worldwide sales of 592,080 vehicles. A whopping 172,731 were sold outside the United States.

The Jeep juggernaut continued into 2012 when it introduced the Pentastar V-6 to the Wrangler and Wrangler Unlimited. The smoother, lighter, more powerful Pentastar engine reduced 0–60 acceleration times from 11.4 to 8.4 seconds, offered fuel economy up to 21 miles per gallon on the highway, and delivered 285 horsepower (up 40 percent) and 260 lb-ft of torque (up 10 percent). Wrangler's upgraded powertrain included a new five-speed automatic transmission. Jeep President/CEO Mike Manley said, "Jeep Wrangler—the most capable and iconic vehicle in the world—has a new heart but retains the same soul for 2012." Wrangler and Unlimited offered four models: Sport, Sport S, Sahara, and Rubicon.

For the 2012 Grand Cherokee line, the Pentastar 3.6-liter V-6 engine on Grand Cherokee offered improved fuel economy and a best-in-class V-6 driving range of more than 500 miles. Aiding fuel economy was the new electro-hydraulic power steering, standard on V-6 models, and a revised automatic transmission for V-8s. With more than forty-five safety features, Grand Cherokee was an Insurance Institute for Highway Safety "Top Safety Pick."

Jeep Compass offered three configurations for 2012: Sport, Latitude, and Limited. All were available with a choice of front-wheel drive, Freedom Drive I, or the Freedom Drive II Off-Road Package. Compass Sport was powered by a 2.0-liter four-cylinder engine producing 158 horsepower mated to a five-speed manual transmission. Standard features included electronic stability control, electronic roll mitigation, Hill-Start Assist, advanced multistage driver and front-seat passenger air bags, side-curtain air bags, plus front driver and passenger active head restraints. Compass Latitude added the continuously variable transmission II (CVT2), remote start, heated front seats, driver seat height adjuster, fold-flat front passenger seat, 60/40 rear seat recline, and leather-wrapped steering wheel with audio and speed controls. Limited models included leather-trimmed seats, four-wheel antilock disc brakes, manual driver lumbar adjust, six-way power driver seat, Electronic Vehicle Information Center, AM/FM/six-disc CD/DVD/MP3/HDD radio, and more. Patriot shared most of the Compass's mechanical improvements.

There were also two special-edition Jeeps for 2012: Wrangler Arctic and Liberty Arctic, featuring winter-themed exteriors and interior designs. "There are few environments more grueling and demanding than the arctic, which is just the type of terrain legendary Jeep vehicles are engineered to conquer," said Manley. "Not

Jeep Grand Cherokee was described as "Adventurously Refined." When equipped with the mighty 5.7-liter Hemi V-8 engine and the awesome Quadra-Drive II four-wheel-drive system with Electronic Limited-Slip Differentials, there was little Mother Nature could send your way that the Jeep couldn't overcome with ease.

only will the Jeep Wrangler Arctic and Jeep Liberty Arctic appeal to our loyal enthusiasts, but their unique content will attract new customers to the Jeep brand."

The Arctic's winter themed colors were Winter Chill, Bright Silver, and Bright White. Exterior features included a body-color hardtop and fender flares, "Arctic" front fender badges, a "Yeti Footprint" decal, black hood decal, and Mopar black fuel filler door and taillamp guards. Liberty Sport Arctic shared many of the same features as Wrangler Arctic. Semigloss black 16-inch aluminum wheels with semigloss black center caps were standard, plus P235/70R16 OWL all-terrain tires. Exterior highlights included deep-tint glass, tow hooks, blacked-out headlamps, and fog lamps. Interiors featured a

black and Arctic Orange color scheme similar to Wrangler's.

With an outstanding product lineup, solid retail network, and an improving economy, sales went through the roof in 2012, with 701,624 Jeeps sold worldwide, a new record. Of that, a noteworthy 227,493 were sold outside the United States. More Jeeps would have been retailed if the company could have produced them, but factories were running beyond their capacity, working overtime trying to keep up with orders.

There was hope Jeep could set another record in 2013, but Liberty went out of production during August 2012 and its replacement wouldn't be ready until the following August. For most of the year Jeep had no midsize SUV.

The popularity of
the Jeep Wrangler
Unlimited four-door
surprised everyone,
especially Jeep product
planners. Over time
it became the best-
selling Wrangler model
and a family favorite.

Liberty's loss made it nearly impossible for Jeep to top 700,000 worldwide sales again, but Manley would try anyway.

The 2013 lineup was good though lacking in novelty. Wrangler Unlimited added a new easy-lift top mechanism and a new premium soft top optionally available on the other Wranglers. New seats with larger bolsters, an auto-dimming mirror with LED map light, new interior lighting, available Alpine speakers, and a tire-pressure monitoring system were other new features. A special-edition Moab offered enhanced off-road capability.

Moab came with 17-inch gloss-black Rubicon alloy wheels, 245/75R17 Goodyear Silent Armor off-road tires, and a Trak-Lok anti-spin rear differential. When equipped with a manual transmission and 3.73 rear axle, Moab boasted a 45:1 crawl ratio. Patriot and Compass models got only a few minor improvements for 2013 and a few new colors.

For 2013, Grand Cherokee Overland Summit models received additional standard features, including front park assist, power folding outside mirrors, and headlight washers. The beautifully finished Overland Summit interior was available with black or saddle Napa leather seating with saddle-accent stitching. There was also an exciting new Grand Cherokee Trailhawk for 2013. Conceptually debuting at the 2012 Easter Jeep Safari in Moab, Utah, the production version came with a choice of V-6 or V-8 and included 18-inch Goodyear Silent Armor tires with Kevlar reinforcement, Rock Rail body protection, electronic limited-slip rear differential (V-8 only), Quadra-Drive II (V-8 only), Quadra-Lift Air Suspension, and Selec-Terrain traction control system. A black hood decal with red accent stripe reduced sun glare. U.S. sales for 2013 dropped to 490,454 vehicles. Business hurt without the Liberty.

Its replacement debuted for 2014 with the resurrection of one of the company's most beloved nameplates: Cherokee. It had a completely new chassis, body, and transmission; two revised engines and three new four-wheel-drive systems; and a unique rear-axle disconnect, among other features.

Base Cherokees had front-wheel drive. Those who preferred four-wheel drive (the vast majority) could choose from Jeep Active Drive I with a single-speed power transfer unit (PTU) (think transfer case), Active Drive II with a two-speed PTU with low range, or Active Drive Lock, which included the two-speed PTU, low range, plus a locking rear differential for severe off-roading. Jeep's Selec-Terrain traction control system offered up to five customized modes: Automatic, Snow, Sport, Sand/Mud, and Rock. Aggressive approach and departure angles provided class-leading off-road capability while superior on-road ride and handling came via a new independent front and rear suspension and increased torsional stiffness. The base engine was Chrysler's 2.4-liter Tigershark MultiAir four-cylinder. A new 3.2-liter Pentastar V-6 was optional.

With best-in-class V-6 towing capability of 4,500 pounds and an available Trail-Rated capability with up to a 56:1 crawl ratio (a 90 percent improvement over Liberty), Cherokee offered up to 31 miles per gallon on the highway. It was the first SUV to offer a nine-speed automatic transmission, and the industry's first rear-axle disconnect system to reduce friction losses and improve fuel efficiency.

Initially the new four-wheel-drive systems experienced problems getting the right degree of smoothness when the axle and driveshaft connected or disconnected. To ensure the rollout wasn't marred by complaints, management quarantined initial production vehicles so each could be individually road-tested and, if necessary, adjusted to the right "feel." It was an immensely costly procedure and introduction was delayed until November 2013 when management was satisfied the vehicle was ready for public release.

Compass and Patriot received a more refined driveline for 2014. The noisy, awkward-shifting continuously variable transmission was replaced by a conventional six-speed automatic providing crisper shifts, improved acceleration, quieter operation, and better highway fuel economy. The duo also got backup cameras, additional sound deadening, and styling updates.

Grand Cherokee got a new eight-speed automatic transmission and a new optional diesel engine. It had long offered a diesel for overseas markets but with increased interest among U.S. consumers, the company decided to offer one in the United States as well.

A new Wrangler Rubicon X special edition for 2014 took off-road capability to a level above the already legendary Rubicon, with a winch-capable bumper, wider rock rails, and additional standard equipment. Included were BFGoodrich KM 255/75R17 tires on 17-inch Rubicon aluminum wheels painted Satin Black with polished faces and a red Jeep Wrangler "icon" logo. Wrangler Freedom Edition returned for 2014 by popular demand. Based on the Sport S, Freedom Editions offered unique exterior and interior trim.

A vintage Cherokee XJ shows its stuff on a tough off-road course.

It all came together to produce a record-breaking year, with U.S. sales soaring to 692,348 vehicles. Jeep was climbing to heights of which they had never dared dream.

The 2015 lineup was the strongest in Jeep's history. The big news was the long-awaited Renegade "small Jeep four-door SUV." Smaller than the Patriot, it was the first Jeep designed on a Fiat chassis, and the first produced in Italy for world markets. Sergio Marchionne's underutilized Fiat factories needed products, and building Renegade there made it more price-competitive in Europe.

Renegade offered four models: Sport, Latitude, Limited, and Trailhawk, the first three in two-wheel and four-wheel-drive versions, the Trailhawk as four-wheel drive only. A 1.4-liter "MultiAir" turbo four-cylinder was standard for Sport and Latitude, with the 2.4-liter Tigershark standard on the others and optional on Sport and Latitude. Boasting best-in-class off-road capability, Renegade was a solid entry into the growing subcompact SUV market.

Cherokee's V-6 for 2015 boasted new "Stop-Start" technology for improved fuel economy. Other new features included "Forward Collision Warning Plus" crash-mitigation support. The ParkView backup camera and automatic headlamps were now standard on Latitude and Trailhawk models, while a new SafetyTec Group featuring blind-spot monitoring and rear cross-path detection—ParkSense rear park assist—and signal mirrors with courtesy lamps was offered on Latitude, Limited, and Trailhawk models.

The 2015 Wrangler got an all-new eight-speaker audio system and improved sound bar as standard (a nine-speaker Alpine system with amplifier and subwoofer optional) and a Torx tool kit for removing the top, doors, and bumper endcaps. The Rubicon Hard Rock Edition, available on Wrangler and Wrangler Unlimited models, was the most capable Wrangler ever. Its part-time four-wheel drive included electronic-locking front and rear Dana 44 axles and a Rock-Trac transfer case with a "4-Low" ratio of 4:1, 4.10 axle ratios front and rear, and Tru-Lok differentials. With a six-speed manual transmission, the Hard Rock Edition boasted an incredible 73.1:1 crawl ratio. Wranglers also offered a new Wheeler Edition with beefed-up hardware, plus dressed-up Freedom Edition models to honor the U.S. military.

Grand Cherokee, the most awarded SUV ever, also received additional content for 2015. Laredo and Limited now featured dark wood trim on the dash and doors. Premium cloth seating was standard on Laredo, while leather came standard on Limited. Grand Cherokee Summit models received added features and a new Summit California Edition appearance package that further enhanced Summit's exterior aesthetics.

Grand Cherokee Summit models received additional standard features including active noise cancellation providing a 10dB noise reduction. There was also the award-winning 3.0-liter EcoDiesel V-6 and eight-speed transmission delivering 30 miles per gallon and best-in-class towing capability of 7,400 pounds. To further enhance Summit's luxury cred, an acoustic laminated windshield and second-row side glass were standard.

With improved models and the new Renegade, Jeep took a giant step forward, selling an incredible 1.23 million vehicles worldwide, including 865,000 in America. Jeep finally had a management smart enough to take advantage of the hottest SUV market in history.

After such a successful launch year there wasn't much new for Cherokee in 2016, aside from new colors and minor enhancements. Engineers continued to fine-tune the drivetrain

The Wrangler Rubicon represents the epitome of the Jeep brand, being the most capable production off-road vehicle you can buy.

For 2013 there was an exciting new Grand Cherokee Trailhawk. First seen as a concept at the 2012 Easter Jeep Safari in Moab, the production Grand Cherokee Trailhawk came with a choice of V-6 or V-8 engines and included rugged features like 18-inch Goodyear Silent Armor tires with Kevlar reinforcement, Rock Rail body protection, Rear Electronic Limited-Slip Differential (V-8 models), Quadra-Drive II (V-8 models), Quadra-Lift air suspension, Selec-Terrain traction control system, and a black hood decal with red accent stripe.

to optimize smoothness. Compass had a similar story for 2016; in its final year before a complete redesign, the model range was cut to just Sport and Latitude. New standard equipment included Uconnect hands-free and SiriusXM Radio. Compass Latitude models got standard automatic headlamps.

For 2016, most Jeep Grand Cherokee models offered improved fuel economy. The 3.6-liter V-6 now included engine stop-start and boasted 295 horsepower. A High-Altitude special edition also debuted. Jeep Renegade offered additional features for 2016, including Beats premium audio, rain-sensing wipers, and new exterior colors. The 2016 Renegade continued to boast best-in-class fuel efficiency and off-road capability. Renegade likewise boasted advanced technology once limited to premium SUVs, including award-winning Uconnect Access,

Uconnect touchscreen radios, and the segment's largest full-color instrument cluster.

For the 2016 Wrangler, Jeep marketers focused on the popular "package" models, adding a Wrangler Black Bear Edition based on the Sport S. In addition, the Rubicon Hard Rock Edition, Freedom Edition, and Willys Wheeler all returned. Wrangler Sahara received new wheels, body-color bumper applique, and an Olive Green interior option.

During the first quarter of 2016, Jeep unveiled unique 75th Anniversary models in every Jeep line. The special-edition vehicles featured unique Jeep Green exteriors, Satin Bronze wheels, Bronze and Orange exterior accents, unique interiors, and anniversary badging.

The overseas business, nurtured for years by Willys-Overland, Kaiser-Jeep, and American Motors, proved significant in 2016. U.S. sales grew to 926,000 units, while worldwide sales grew to 1.4 million vehicles!

As the 2017 model year arrived, management was beginning to execute a plan for relocating production of many of its vehicles to substantially boost Jeep production. Cherokee assembly was moved out of the Toledo North plant and into the completely renovated Belvidere Assembly Plant 60 miles west of Chicago. Wrangler would move from the cramped Toledo Supplier Park facility to the much larger Toledo North Plant where the company could significantly increase production. Grand Cherokee production remained in Detroit.

A new 2017 Jeep Compass debuted, engineered to surpass the first-generation Compass in every area. Based on a lengthened Renegade platform, Jeep claimed the Compass was the "Most capable compact SUV ever," boasting the most advanced 4x4 systems in its class: Jeep Active Drive and Active Drive w/Low Range. Models sold in North America came with the 2.4-liter Tigershark, delivering over 30 miles per gallon. A global product, Compass would be manufactured in Brazil, China, Mexico, and India and sold in more than 100 countries.

The 2017 Wrangler and Wrangler Unlimited models got new LED headlights and fog lamps: optional on Sport and Sport S, standard on Sahara and Rubicon. A new Cold Weather Group offered on Sport S and Rubicon models included 17-inch BFGoodrich KO2 tires, engine-block heater, slush mats, Power Convenience Group, heated seats, and remote start. In February, Jeep unveiled the Wrangler Rubicon Recon Edition, which upped the off-road ante with a front axle upgrade featuring strengthened tubes and heavy-duty end forgings, heavy-duty cast front and rear differential covers, enhanced rock rails, part-time four-wheel drive with electronic-locking front and rear, Dana 44 axles, and a Rock-Trac transfer case with a 4-Low ratio of 4:1. A 4.10 front and rear axle ratio was standard along with Tru-Lok differentials. Also unveiled in 2017, the Wrangler Chief Edition was painted bright blue with a white hardtop, a white side stripe, and vintage-looking spoke wheels, mimicking the classic 1974–1983 J-series Cherokee Chief.

Grand Cherokee offered only carryover models until April 2017 when Jeep introduced a new Grand Cherokee Trackhawk. Considered a 2018 model, it boasted an incredible 707 horsepower, courtesy of its supercharged 6.2-liter V-8. Grand Cherokee, already the most awarded and most capable full-size SUV on the planet, was now also the most powerful and quickest ever built. This benchmark engine was combined with a beefed-up high-torque capacity TorqueFlite eight-speed automatic transmission and enhanced chassis. Performance was insane: 0–60 in 3.5 seconds, and a top speed of 180 miles per hour. Despite the success of the Trackhawk, Jeep sales slipped a bit in 2017 to 1.388 million worldwide.

In 2018, the all-new Wrangler JL represented a leap forward in technology, with lightweight, high-strength aluminum doors, hinges, hood, fenders, and windshield frame, plus a magnesium swing-gate all helping to reduce weight and boost fuel economy. Suspension tuning optimized Wrangler's on-road handling and ride without sacrificing off-road capability. Engine choices included an all-new 2.0-liter turbocharged four-cylinder with eTorque technology, a 3.6-liter Pentastar V-6 with Engine Stop-Start, and beginning in 2019, a 3.0-liter EcoDiesel V-6 with ESS. Two transmissions were offered: a new eight-speed automatic and a six-speed manual. Wrangler two-door models were available in three configurations: Sport, Sport S,

and Rubicon. Wrangler four-door models came in four: Sport, Sport S, Sahara, and Rubicon.

The 2018 Cherokee saw realigned trim levels and enhanced standard equipment. Latitude was now the base model and included standard 17-inch aluminum wheels, fog lamps, and high-intensity discharge headlamps, roof rails, backup camera, and body-color mirrors and door handles. A new Latitude Plus trim added standard Uconnect radio with color touch screen, SiriusXM Radio, Passive Entry/Keyless Go, cloth seats with leather inserts, leather steering wheel, eight-way power driver seat, and more. Cherokee Trailhawk and Cherokee Limited were also upgraded.

For 2019, Cherokee was produced at Belvidere, which underwent a $350 million overhaul to modernize and increase capacity, creating approximately 300 new jobs. Cherokee was given a facelift; new headlamps were mounted in a more normal position, replacing the widely criticized low-mounted headlamps. Compass Sport added a new Upland high-trim edition, while Renegade got minor styling updates and a new 1.3-liter direct-injection turbo four.

Toward the end of 2018, Jeep unveiled its upcoming 2020 Wrangler-based Gladiator pickup that enthusiasts had been requesting for years. By relocating Wrangler production to Toledo North, Jeep finally was able to produce the Gladiator.

The rest of the 2020 Jeep line boasted impressive updates. The Wrangler lineup included four models: Sport, Sport S, Sahara (four-door only), and Rubicon. The Wrangler featured an updated powertrain menu. Available on Wrangler Sport and Rubicon were a 2.0-liter four-cylinder with ESS technology, a 3.6-liter ESS V-6 and, later in the year, a 3.0-liter EcoDiesel ESS with a thumping 442 lb-ft of torque. Sahara models offered the 3.6-liter ESS (manual shift only), a 2.0-liter mild-hybrid with eTorque assist, a 3.6-liter mild-hybrid with eTorque assist, and the 3.0-liter EcoDiesel ESS. Wrangler Sport and Rubicon now offered the 2.0-liter ESS turbocharged inline four. The 3.6-liter Pentastar V-6 with mild-hybrid eTorque technology was available exclusively on Wrangler Sahara.

Three new trim levels also debuted: the Wrangler Willys, Freedom, and Black & Tan editions. Willys Editions included a limited-slip rear differential, rock rails, and aggressive 32-inch Mud Terrain tires plus special decals. The Freedom Edition was designed as a tribute to U.S. military members with military-themed design cues. The Black & Tan boasted special exterior and interior content, including a premium tan soft top, black exterior badging, and special accents. LED headlamps and fog lights were a new option on Sport models.

The 2020 Grand Cherokee Trackhawk featured a yellow-accented Trackhawk badge on the liftgate, 20-inch titanium aluminum wheels, and the Signature Leather-Wrapped Interior Package in Black/Ski Gray. Grand Cherokee Limited and Trailhawk models now included a standard single-pane sunroof. A new Premium Lighting Group available on Grand Cherokee Laredo, Limited, and Trailhawk included bi-xenon high-intensity discharge (HID) headlamps, signature daytime running lights, LED fog lamps, and automatic high-beam headlamps.

Jeep's new Active Safety Group was available on Grand Cherokee Laredo and included Forward Collision Warning Plus, LaneSense Lane Departure Warning Plus, auto high-beam headlamps, and advanced brake assist.

Cherokee for 2020 boasted an optional Advanced Safety Group that included Lane Departure Warning Plus, Forward Collision Warning Plus, and rain-sensing wipers available on select models. Also new were Alexa Skill Technology available on Uconnect 4C/4C NAV with 8.4-inch display, Sangria and Spitfire Orange exterior paint colors, and 19-inch wheels available for the Limited.

Compass Sport for 2020 offered an optional Safety & Security Group that included Gloss Black exterior mirrors, blind-spot monitoring with rear cross path detection, ParkSense rear park assist system, rain-sensing windshield

This 2019 Wrangler Unlimited is fitted with a snorkel to allow it to traverse deeper streams. The bright oval forms in the JL's standard front bumper received criticism from some shoppers. *Chris Collard*

wipers, and vehicle theft alarm. Also available was the Advanced Safety Group with leather steering wheel, Forward Collision Warning Plus, Lane Departure Warning Plus, auto high-beam headlamps, adaptive cruise control, advanced brake assist, and auto-dimming rearview mirror.

Finally, the 2020 Renegade offered a Kenwood premium audio nine-speaker system, Safety & Security Group with blind-spot monitoring and rear cross path detection, rain-sensing windshield wipers, security alarm, and tonneau cover (available on Sport/Upland models). An LED Lighting Group (LED headlamps, daytime running lamps, taillamps, fog lamps) became available on Latitude models with 2.4-liter engines. Renegade also boasted a new Advanced Tech Group (Forward Collision Warning Plus with Mitigation, Lane Departure Warning Plus with Lane Keep Assist, adaptive cruise control, ParkSense Parallel/Perpendicular Park Assist with front and rear park sensors, automatic high-beam headlamps) optional on Latitude models with the 2.4-liter engine and on Sport models.

As of 2020, Jeep vehicles were manufactured in the United States, Mexico, Brazil, Venezuela, Italy, Egypt, China, and India. Jeep truly is America's most recognized and beloved vehicle—a world-class wonder machine.

INDEX